Through *the* Garden Gate

QUILTERS AND THEIR GARDENS

JEAN & VALORI WELLS

C&T PUBLISHING

VALORI WELLS:

GARDEN PORTRAITIST

As you travel from one garden to another,
whether you enjoy an orderly paradise,
a whimsical setting, or a close-up view,
you have Valori Wells to thank for her
vision and interpretation. She spent
many hours shooting, and then selecting
the many images to capture that special
essence she felt in each garden.
Respectfully, the creators of these
environments provided her with settings
worth exploring with her camera.

Developmental Editor: Barbara Konzak Kuhn

Technical Editor: Joyce Engels Lytle

Cover Design: Christina Jarumay

Book Design: Christina Jarumay

Illustrator: Jay Richards © C&T Publishing

Quilt photographer: Ross Chandler

Print photography (pages 96 - 97): Gary Alvis, Studio 7 Photography

Garden photography: Valori Wells

Attention Teachers: C&T Publishing, Inc. encourages you to use this book as a text for teaching. Contact us at 800-284-1114 or www.ctpub.com for more information about the C&T Teachers Program.

Jean's Stitch Thread is a trademark of YLI.

Starbucks Coffee is a registered trademark of Starbucks Corporation.

Library of Congress Cataloging-in-Publication Data

Wells, Jean.

    Through the garden gate: quilters and their gardens / Jean Wells and Valori Wells.

    p.   cm.

    Includes index.

    ISBN 1-57120-065-7 (pbk.)

    1. Quilting--Patterns. 2. Patchwork--Patterns. 3. Appliqué--Patterns. 4. Gardens in art. I. Wells, Valori. II. Title.

TT835.W4656   1999

746.46'041--dc21   98-45278

                  CIP

Published by C&T Publishing, Inc.

P.O. Box 1456

Lafayette, California 94549

Printed in Hong Kong

10 9 8 7 6 5 4 3

ACKNOWLEDGMENTS

We wish to acknowledge the following people who have made *Through the Garden Gate* the beautiful book that it is.

All of the quilters who graciously let us share their gardens and quilting experiences...

The C&T Publishing family for believing in our idea and developing it into a fine book.

Barbara Kuhn for her superb job as the developmental editor. Her guidance and expertise helped to portray the gardens and quilts in the manner we intended.

It was a pleasure to work again with Diane Pedersen. Her "artistic fine tuning" adds so much to C&T books.

A how-to book without expert technical editing would be a disaster. Joyce Lytle is the very best and we appreciate her efforts.

Jay Richards for doing a great job illustrating our sketches.

Our applause to Christina Jarumay for one of her first book designs. What a joy to see her fresh ideas; her work with the color and graphics makes the book sing.

The Stitchin' Post staff for their understanding and encouragement.

Katrina Beverage for always working us into her schedule and for her machine quilting expertise.

John and Henry for their love, support, and understanding of "artistically temperamental" women.

All of the gardeners and quilters who continue to inspire us all.

DEDICATION

In memory of
Sara Lee Morse Butler

...Jean's mother and Valori's grandmother, who always tended her roses and had ones named for each family member.

PREFACE

Growing a garden is the art of grafting nature's wonder onto our yearning for beauty. The effort requires equal parts of fantasy, toil, and trickery. And when the weather is risky, prayer too.

These days we fashion gardens as extensions of ourselves. Like quilts, most gardens have evolved beyond function. No longer necessary as a food source, most gardens have become private sanctuaries, sources of nurture for the spirit. We know the magic that happens when we physically step into and surround our whole selves with beauty. In our private melodrama, we become the dogwood blossoms, the fragrance of lavender, the dallying butterfly. Momentarily we are transformed.

To fully appreciate a beautiful garden, one can never hurry the experience. Instead, we yield to nature's rhythm, and wait for the garden to reveal itself gradually. In lingering, we increase our capacity to savor details—to be enchanted by them, to be surprised by them. A beautiful garden waits to be discovered slowly, and does not give itself away in a single glance. Assorted features in the landscape lead us from one to another, tugging at us with new enticements. If the enticements also defy our expectation, then our appreciation is enlarged to include a sense of wonder.

Knowing these things, we intentionally cultivate gardens with the hope of sustaining the promise of their succor. Barren spaces are transformed into welcoming places that can dazzle the eye or simply refresh it. Although cultivation is preparation for an eventual reward, sincere gardeners are rewarded more often through the work itself. The digging, the arranging, the watering—these tasks become instruments of personal transformation. Many who garden organically recognize the work of creating a garden as natural therapy.

Because we acknowledge nature's basic law that everything changes, we experience a oneness with beauty, where there is also a gratifying recognition of good fortune. Right time, right place—what luck! Hence, in gaining access to a stranger's garden, the feeling of good fortune accompanies us. Sheepishly too, it must be admitted, that our anticipation is also laden with voyeuristic thrill. None can resist the temptation to tread in someone else's garden.

A gate is an acknowledged boundary between the public and the private. The invitation to step beyond the garden gate is a privilege. We imagine the earthly delights that await us, and we cherish this hospitality. To be privy to the revelations of beautiful gardens is a gift. We are beholden to these gardeners for inviting us to pass through their garden gates. What luck!

Andrea Balosky
author of *Transitions*

TABLE OF CONTENTS

INTRODUCTION

Through the Garden Gate

Which comes first: gardening or quilting, or do the interests develop simultaneously? The intertwining of ideas between one and the other make these interests alike in many ways. *Through the Garden Gate* explores quilting and gardening from the initial planning stages to the intimacy of detail in a single flower, or in the combination of quilting stitches on the quilt surface. Whether you like to garden and are looking for themes and inspiration, or you are a quilter looking for color and design ideas, you will find this book full of possibilities.

As we visit each quilter in his or her garden, special qualities become evident, personalities emerge—each creator communicates a personal vision. We knew our contributors through their quilts. Just as each quilt exhibits a strong sense of personality, these same personalities emerge as we walk along garden paths. With the photographic images and commentaries that follow, we share the personalities we experienced in our visits so that you can gain insight into the intricacies of the garden and the intimacy of the quilting.

Gardens are a place to express ideas for color and design. Consider the fifty-two varieties of lavender cultivated by Roxy Burgard at her farmhouse, then portrayed in the *Lavender Patch* quilt. The color choices were a natural for someone intimately involved in her garden. As Roxy told us "I sew the patches of my life...the light and the dark! In my garden I work among both the flowers and the weeds. All make up the complex patchwork of a lifetime." What is sown outside not only creates a landscape out-of-doors but comes inside and finds itself in fabric palettes that continue on to the next quilt in a series of life experiences.

Imagine the colors of Freddy Moran's garden when you look at *Just Us Chickens*. Freddy plants her garden just as she stitches images in her quilts. With this gardener a strong sense of color is played up in her surroundings. When we visited her home, we found more than thirty different colors on the walls, ceiling, floors, and woodwork. I would know her house anywhere, just as I can always recognize a "Freddy" quilt by its vibrant colors and intricate play of black and white.

Catherine and Mel Bryan's garden became the setting for the wedding of Edie and Bob Hines. Quilting has many similarities to gardening, and both can act as a metaphor for marriage. First it is imagined—then it is created! The process is like exploring the unknown with good friends. It is a journey. Here the promise of what's to come in a garden or quilt is revealed as magic; yet that magic doesn't happen all at once—it is ongoing, just as a garden, a quilt, or a marriage grows.

Gardens and quilts alike are stories, each unique with its own theme, one which reflects the interests and vision of the creator. Much is to be learned from studying these quilts and techniques and applying the lessons learned to your own garden setting. *Through the Garden Gate* is meant to be used as inspiration: the text is developed to assist you in your own growth as a gardener and quilter. Enjoy!

Jean Wells

FROM THE GARDEN TO THE QUILT

Along the Path to Creativity

se each chapter, featuring a different quilter's garden along with the commentary and photographs, as inspiration for your quiltmaking journeys. Let the elements of a garden landscape inspire you, or use the colors to enhance a current project. A single flower may even start you collecting fabrics for a future quilt.

 DESIGN PROCESS

Begin by exploring your ideas. Ideas are everywhere, but you have to look. By becoming familiar with something, you will learn about how it might be interpreted. Compare how paths, walkways, or stepping stones might relate to sashing in a quilt; how a row of perennials relates to a border on a quilt, or how a vase of roses might translate into a quilt design of simple Nine-Patch blocks. Look at individual plants closely. Study the play of color, line, and texture. Every plant and every fabric has a role in this process. Even that fabric bought on impulse from the 70's might find a home in a garden quilt. Keep your mind open to the possibilities of every piece of fabric.

Each of the contributors in *Through the Garden Gate* has interpreted individual flowers, foliage, or an overall garden in his or her quilt design. You can learn from these people as their experiences help you in interpreting your particular idea. Study the quilts and gardens to learn how to design on a variety of levels.

VISION

What sets your imagination running? For Tonye Phillips, it is the bright faces of summer flowers she portrayed in *Flower Power*. Valori Wells re-created in *Memories of My Mother's Garden* the fond elements of a garden she has known since childhood. A vision must come into place before you will be ready to design your quilt. Just as gardens range from small patches to acres of trees and flowers, so too do quilts differ in appearance. A single concept may develop in a wall quilt, whereas many concepts come together in a large bed quilt. Let your vision grow and change as you progress down the design path.

Analyze pictures and garden scenes. You will learn to "see" beyond the obvious to the details. And to see textures as well as color. Look at the lines in the textures–are they jagged, curvy, flowing, straight? What details can you identify? Can you find fabrics to interpret these textures? Have fun with your imagination. Dream a little! Once an idea starts to form, simplify. This means taking it down to its basic shape. How might you interpret it? Rely on familiar, simple pieced blocks or combinations of blocks and appliqué to get your idea across. Remember, unless you want to make an exact replica of the scene to appliqué, you are creating an impression with color, line, and design.

What major elements do you want to portray in the picture? Will it be the color of the lettuce leaves in *Tossed Salad*? Or the flowers, foliage, and bugs in *Enchanted Morning*? Is it a scene on an actual backyard fence in *Uncle Sam Lives Here*? Or is it the subtle colors of roses in *Vanilla Rose*? Once you start making some of these decisions, the quilt design will start taking shape.

Fabric choices will make or break a great design. Study your fabric—see its unique qualities. What can it be besides the obvious? In *Uncle Sam Lives Here*, Margaret Peters looked at printed fabric for the individual elements she wanted to portray to create her quilt. Catherine Bryan was able to work the color values and have a vase of roses emerge by using the Double Nine-Patch quilt design from *Quilts! Quilts!! Quilts!!!* by Laura Nownes and Diana McClun.

STYLE

Through the Garden Gate is designed as an inspirational interpretation of color and design for quilters as well as gardeners. Style is evident within each of the different gardens. Some are lush orderly paradises while others are whimsical and casual. Even a mystical quality is evident in Gwen Marston's natural island setting.

Identify the style you like: whether formal, structured, informal, or whimsical. Now look for simple pieced blocks that might work for the design. I find that simpler piecing better allows a design to develop into a garden concept. A complicated quilt design along with complicated subject matter creates a confused quilt design—one where the maker's vision is not evident. The viewer will question, what is more important, the piecing style or the composition?

Ponder these points before you start designing a quilt. Or adapt the theme of one of the quilts in *Through the Garden Gate* to your garden using the colors and textures that you see every day.

GRAPH PAPER

Graph paper comes in handy during the design stage. Sketching the design helps to corral the idea and find a repeat pattern if there is one. A good example is found in Valori's quilt, *Memories of My Mother's Garden*. By putting ideas on graph paper, she realized it would add more interest to use more block sizes besides the 10" x 10" and 5" x 5". When designing on graph paper, you will soon find out if all of the pieces will fit together. Another value is seeing everything in proportion to each other, especially if one area is large and unbalanced by the other blocks.

COLLECTING FABRICS

Pictures help this process, since they act to remind you of the vision. But not all pictures need be of gardens. Color ideas can come from dishes, fabrics, etc. Not only should you collect pictures, but you should collect fabrics that might work for the vision. This is an ongoing process and should be treated as such. Very seldom do I find all the fabrics in one outing. I build the collection. For me this is an exciting part of the journey. I also remember where one fabric was purchased, or if a friend shared from her collection. Choose a variety of values in the different color groups. Look for styles, such as wood textures, petal shapes, or transition fabrics that segue from sky to foliage colors. Consider what the fabric print can be besides what it actually is. Then, envision it cut up.

COLOR AND TEXTURE

Carefully study the colors that are evident in the picture. Identify not only the color family but also study the values in the color families, identifying the lights, medium-lights, mediums, medium-darks, and darks.

Study the relationship of the colors next to each other.

Ask yourself, "Why do they work?" Is there anything that you would alter? Make notes on what might be pleasing to the eye. You are the creator. Note what percentage of the picture is green, pink, white, etc. By determining the same proportions, you are setting yourself up for a good composition. If the colors work in the same proportion as in the picture, they will work in your quilt. Collect a lot of fabrics so that you have choices when it comes to composing the quilt. Remember these fabrics are auditioning for the quilt. They won't all find a place in the design.

Look at the textures shown in your photographs and try to find similar textural moods in the fabrics that you choose. You will need fabrics with movement and those that have a calming effect. A place to rest the eye always helps the composition.

Transition fabrics help bridge the color areas from one another. A fabric with blue and green might work for sky to foliage areas, or a pink and green fabric for transition from flower to leaves. These fabrics, when carefully used, will help the design to look like a garden.

Use an accent color in the composition. An accent color is a small amount of a higher contrast color that sparks the design. As I studied the colors in the lettuce last summer, I came to realize that the reddish hue at the tips of the lime-green leaves made the whole patch look lively. Then there were the soft purple and mauve tones contrasting with the bright greens and they all blended beautifully. Learn from Mother Nature!

REPETITION CREATES UNITY

Repetition of elements in quilt design creates unity. Although the repeated block designs or units is one form of repetition, the fabrics in the block designs don't necessarily need to be repeated. You might repeat the shapes of elements in the quilt. Rhythm in more contemporary designs is created when elements are repeated. Colors and combinations of colors are automatically repeated elements. Another opportunity to repeat is in the quilting pattern. Thought and planning of the repeating units will unify the design.

FINISHING TOUCHES

BORDERS OR NOT

Borders are an integral part of the quilt design, as much as they are an integral part of the garden. A border added haphazardly can ruin a good design, whereas a good border can extend the design elements as it does in *Vanilla Rose*. A border can frame a vision as in *Summer Garden*, or a border might not be necessary, as in *Tossed Salad*, and the design can stand alone.

Consider carefully the quilt design when planning a border. Try different fabrics or combinations of fabrics in different widths. Sometimes the quilt will work if you change the width of a border by an inch. Remember to please the quilt first.

A $1/4$" seam allowance is used throughout the book.

BATTING AND LAYERING

For a wall hanging, choose a flat batting so the quilt lies flat when hung. For a bed quilt, choose a batting with more loft since the quilt will be draped over the mattress. Both batting and backing should be 2" larger than the quilt top on each side. When layering the quilt, first secure the backing with clamps or masking tape to keep it taut. This will ensure that you don't get bubbles on the back when you quilt. Gently pat out the batting over the backing. Lay the top over the batting, centering and aligning the edges parallel so they don't ripple. It is well worth it to take the time and be patient during this part of quiltmaking, so the end result will be better. Baste with safety pins or needle and thread to secure the layers.

QUILTING DESIGNS

Plan the quilting design to further enhance your original vision. Think through the ideas and if necessary draw them on tracing paper, then place them over the quilt to see if you like them. Look for elements to repeat in the quilting stitches.

Tonye Phillip's love of hand quilting further enhanced her original vision in *Flower Power*. Around the random flower centers, Tonye portrayed a variety of different flower petals, then cleverly quilted the names of her sons, Ande and Charlie, on their favorite flowers, then did the same for her husband, Doug, and her own name, Tonye Belinda. What better way to personalize a quilt! The quilted vines in the sashing and borders are reminiscent of the hop vines that cover her greenhouse and trellis. These flowing vines complement the flower designs and add the final touch. Or follow the example set by Kathy Sandbach when she used variegated thread to quilt leaf lines in Freddy Moran's *Just Us Chickens*. The variegated thread repeats the melody of colors in the quilt while the rambling leaf pattern adds a garden touch.

QUILTING

Notice that many of the quilts have quilting lines that cross over the seams. The piecing then becomes a backdrop that is enhanced by the quilting. However, when quilting over intricately pieced quilts, too many seams may make hand quilting difficult. For these quilts, you should rely on machine quilting. For most quilts, either machine or hand quilting—or a combination of both—is acceptable.

BINDING

Binding style is a very individual decision. There are many methods, and each has its own merit. A very simple method is given below:

1. Cut binding strips 1 $3/4$" wide on the cross grain of the fabric. Stitch strips together if you need strips longer than 40".

2. Matching the raw edge of the quilt to one edge of the binding strip, stitch the binding to the quilt, right sides together, using a $1/4$" seam allowance. I like to use the walking, or even feed foot when sewing the binding on to keep the fabric from creating puckers. Trim batting and backing to the $1/4$" seam allowance.

3. Turn under the remaining raw edge $1/4$" and press. Slipstitch the pressed edge to the back of the quilt.

4. Repeat steps 1-3 for the remaining edges, finishing the corners as shown.

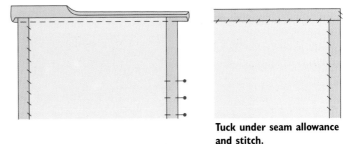

Tuck under seam allowance and stitch.

For other binding ideas, refer to your favorite quilting books.

As you journey through these gardens and experience the quilting creations, we hope you'll be inspired to create ones of your own—and that you'll share them with us.

Jean and Valori

JEAN WELLS: Wild & whimsical

Wild and whimsical are the best adjectives to describe this unusual garden. It has an essence all its own and is self directed. At its start eighteen years ago, several varieties of daisies were planted in a rock-edged flower bed, but this was just the beginning. The daisies returned year after year to be joined by gloriosa daisies, bachelor buttons, California poppies, a wide variety of perennials, and wildflowers of all kinds. A composition of willow, sage brush, pine, and juniper trees form the transitional forest which surrounds the garden.

The life of the garden today is ever-changing. In the fall, the flowers go to seed as the foliage covers the ground. As the weather turns colder, snow creates a blanket that protects the seeds until spring. In the springtime, when the warm sun returns and the rocks heat up, the seeds germinate. They are either left to grow where they sprout or are later moved to other areas or given to friends. This is how the garden has grown from one small flower bed to a setting that extends over two acres. Wildflower seeds, resown every couple of years, add extra color and variety—with these mavericks you never know what will come up from year to year.

 Many of the wildflowers, such as the lupine, have established themselves and return larger and larger every year. Beside the roots of an overturned tree lives a wild yellow rose that came to Oregon many generations ago with Jean's relatives via the Oregon Trail. Starts from it continue to be passed on from one generation to the next. Most mornings during the late spring, summer, and fall, you will see Jean with her basket and scissors cutting flowers for vases in her stores, The Stitchin' Post and The Wild Hare. Inside her house the tables are covered with vases of flowers. The flower arrangements change with the seasons but follow the same style as the garden—wild and whimsical!

For this quilter, gardening has become a spiritual experience as well as a creative and entertaining one. Time in the garden, whether it is spent digging out the never-ending cheat grass, or watering plants, designing a new area, raking pine needles, and dead-heading flowers, is time that feeds the soul. If you ask Jean, she will tell you that weeding a flower bed can be an experience where problems are solved and challenges sort themselves out.

The creative process in both gardening and quilting involves hard work and extensive decision-making, but the results are well worth the effort. You are constantly dealing with texture, shape, and color, and considering the light source. In quilting and gardening you get results. For Jean it is time spent away from her bustling businesses that gives her something to show for her efforts. Gardening becomes her inspiration as she gathers ideas for quilts that will be made in the fall and winter, after the garden is put to bed. Quilting ideas flow in these months and the summer garden is re-created in fabric. In this way Jean carries her love of flowers throughout the year.

Jean adds, "It's a treat to sit by the creek and watch the birds bathing themselves and listen to the wind blowing through the pine trees. I look up at the clear blue sky and realize that it just doesn't get any better than this. I've created my own private environment with the help of Mother Nature. It is my refuge."

What a joy to harvest the fruits of your efforts in a vegetable garden. The feeling of being able to grow something and enjoy the pleasures of the palate, as well as experience the visual impact, is a spiritual experience for many a gardener. When late fall arrives, Jean digs potatoes and harvests leeks for soup, then starts dreaming of the vegetable garden to be planted next spring. In her mind it seems she is either planting gardens or stitching quilts. Jean enjoys connecting with the soil as well as with fabric and color in quilts.

It took several tries for the vegetable garden to become what it is today. A former dog kennel was fitted with three raised rectangular flower beds. The first year of planting most of the seeds didn't germinate and only the cheat grass grew in abundance. Last year, Jean consulted with master gardener Jerry Balosky and found that the dirt needed compost and nutrients. With Jerry's assistance the vegetable garden became a reality and vegetables grew in abundance. "I could hardly pick the lettuce it was so beautiful and I didn't want to spoil the visual impact. A friend came to visit and as we strolled in the garden she said the lettuce positively called out for dressing."

Tossed Salad

After experiencing the bountiful summer garden, all Jean could think of was creating a "lettuce quilt." The colors and textures were vivid in her mind. Scanning through quilt books for inspiration, Jean happened upon an antique Log Cabin quilt where the blocks were set on point. The setting created rows of light and dark that resembled the rows of a garden. Jean decided on using a six-inch Log Cabin block, set on point, and immediately knew how the quilt would look. Little splashes of deep reds, wine, and purple were the essential accent with all of the greens just as they were in the garden.

Jean took fabrics out to the garden and auditioned them for the quilt, then she matched colors and textures to the lettuce. As the design progressed, she placed accent red and purple fabrics back and forth between the light and dark side of the quilt. These accents carry the eye across the surface, just as the red and purple colors do in the garden. All of the design and color clues for the quilt were taken from this first vegetable garden. Then, when Jean was working on the quilt at a Stitchin' Post retreat, a student walked by and ran her hand through the strips Jean had piled on the sewing table. The student said, "tossed salad," which became the title of the quilt.

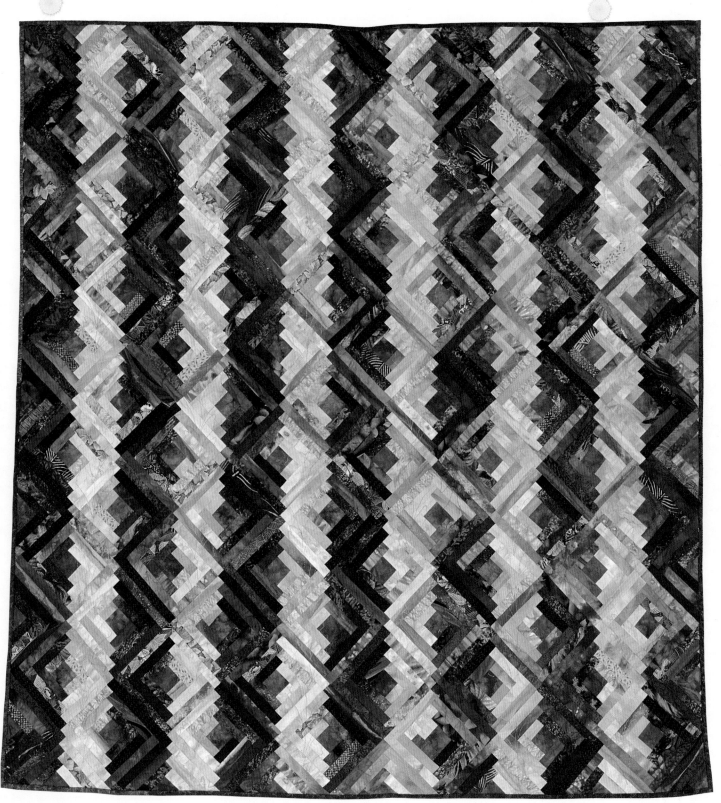

JEAN WELLS

Quilted by Katrina Beverage

55 ¹/₄" x 59 ¹/₂"

❀ TOSSED SALAD

❀ MATERIALS

- ²/₃ yard green for centers
- 2 ¼ yards of assorted greens for light areas
- 2 ½ yards of assorted greens for dark areas
- ¼ yard scraps for accent colors (reds and purples)
- 3 ½ yards for binding and backing
- 59" x 63" batting

❀ CUTTING

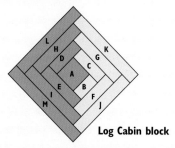

Log Cabin block

For center **A**, cut green fabric into 2" strips, then cut strips into 103 squares. For pieces **B-M**, cut all light, dark, and accent fabrics into 1 ¼" strips.

❀ DIRECTIONS

A chart is given to show the length of each strip in the block. You can pre-cut the strip lengths, mixing up the fabrics in the dark and light areas, tossing in accents, or picking strips at random and cutting them off as you stitch. Jean used the latter method, making four to six blocks at a time. As you can see when they are randomly placed in the quilt, no two look alike.

Light areas		Dark areas	
B	2"	**D**	2 ³/₄"
C	2 ³/₄"	**E**	3 ½"
F	3 ½"	**H**	4 ¼"
G	4 ¼"	**I**	5"
J	5"	**L**	5 ³/₄"
K	5 ³/₄"	**M**	6 ½"

1. Place **A** and **B** together, with right sides together, and stitch along one edge. As you near the end of the seam, pick up another **A** and **B** and feed both into the machine as you finish the first set. Chain four sets together.

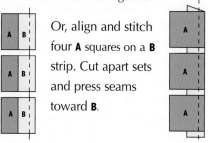

Or, align and stitch four **A** squares on a **B** strip. Cut apart sets and press seams toward **B**.

A strip is under B   **B strip is under A**

2. Pick up **C** and place **A B** on top of it. Stitch as shown. Press toward **C**.

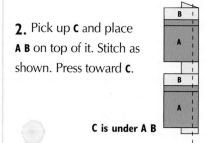

C is under A B

3. Pick up **D** and stitch as shown. Press toward **D**.

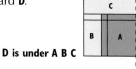

D is under A B C

4. Pick up **E** and stitch as shown. Press toward **E**.

E is under A B C D

5. You have completed one round. You will see light strips on two sides of the center and dark strips on the other two sides. Follow this same color pattern throughout the construction of the block, inserting an accent fabric at random.

6. Make 103 blocks. Arrange blocks on point in rows as shown. Half of the outer blocks will be trimmed off to make a straight edge on the quilt. Scraps from cutting off the edges will be inserted for the left-hand top and bottom corners.

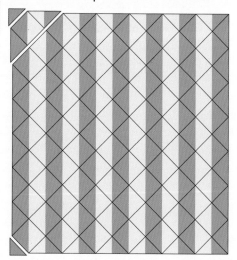

7. Stitch each row together in a diagonal set. Press. Join the rows. Press.

8. Stitch a line through the middle of the outer blocks to mark the edge of the quilt. This stay-stitching line will also stabilize the edge of the quilt. Trim the excess from the blocks, $^{1}/_{4}$" from the stitching line.

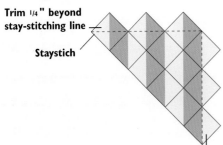

Trim $^{1}/_{4}$" beyond stay-stitching line

Staystich

9. From the excess block material, select two pieces to complete the left-hand top and bottom corners of the quilt. Cut the corner triangles as shown, and attach to the quilt. Press.

Corner triangles for left side of quilts

4 $^{1}/_{4}$"   6"

4 $^{1}/_{4}$"

❀ FINISHING

Refer to the Batting and Layering instructions on page 13. A quilting template was designed using the shape of lettuce leaves. To use the template provided on page 123, first photocopy the design then glue it to medium-weight cardstock. Cut the template. Trace the design onto the quilt with a marking pencil of your choice, then machine or hand quilt the design. The lettuce leaf design was quilted in one direction on the dark areas and in the opposite direction on the light areas. Refer to the Binding instructions on page 13.

Arnie the Supervisor, Jean's garden kitty

Memories of My Mother's Garden

After spending the summer photographing many beautiful and unique gardens, it was finally Valori's turn to make a quilt. "My mind was overflowing with images and possibilities," explains Valori, "Yet, my move in February to Greensboro, North Carolina had made me a little home-sick and I found myself on a deadline to complete the quilt. In my heart was my mother's garden, which had been influencing my life and work for years. My wish was to create a quilt I could give to Mom as thanks for her teaching me to love flowers and quilting. My mother, Jean Wells, has been such a wonderful teacher and mother that it was the least I could do. Although I was a beginning quilter (with advanced ideas) I wanted to find a block that was fun so I wouldn't get too frustrated in the process. I decided to design my blocks using the sew-and-flip method of foundation piecing, which Mom had taught me the previous summer.

I began sketching my basic idea on graph paper: the sun, the moon, and the Three Sisters Mountains on the top of the design, with trees running down the sides separated by mint-colored fabric. Next I drew the flower garden (which became the middle) and then the pond and rocks on the bottom.

The basic quilt plan is a grid using a 5" repeat. Some blocks are 2¹/₂" x 10", and some are 5" x 10". I knew everything had to fit together eventually, but by starting with a variety of squares and rectangles I was able to expand on my ideas and personalize the garden scene. I was also able to create impressions of the sun, moon, mountains, and garden flowers by varying the cutting of the pieces using the sew-and-flip technique. I found, as a lot of quilters do, that things changed as I worked. My quilt grew and took shape as did the gardens of this book—over time and with a lot of love and patience."

VALORI WELLS

60" × 75"

✿ MEMORIES OF MY MOTHER'S GARDEN

✿ MATERIALS

Using the sew-and-flip technique is a piece-as-you-go way of working, so general amounts of fabric are given for piecing. You will find that with this method each person has his or her own way of cutting.

- 3 yards muslin for foundation (Approximate yardage amounts are given for the values in the quilt.) Collect fabrics for the individual elements in the quilt—the mountains, the zinnias, etc. Fat quarters (18" x 22") work well except for the border strips, where 40"-wide yardage is preferred.
- 1 1/2 yards of darks for sky, mountains, ground, trees, foliage, first border, and bottom border
- 1 yard medium darks for sky, trees, mountains, foliage, and flowers
- 1 yard medium lights for flowers, foliage, mountains, moon, and second border
- 1 yard brights for sun and flowers
- 1/2 yard binding
- 3 1/2 yard backing
- 67" x 79" batting

✿ CUTTING

For foundation pieces, cut the following blocks from muslin.

- five 10 1/2" x 10 1/2"
- two 10 1/2" x 15 1/2"
- fourteen 5 1/2" x 10 1/2"
- twenty-nine 5 1/2" x 5 1/2"
- twelve 3" x 10 1/2"

For the first border, cut five strips 2" x 40". Stitch strips together lengthwise. Cut sides 55 1/2", and the top and bottom 38 1/2".

For the second border, cut five strips 1 1/2" x 40". Stitch strips together lengthwise. Cut sides 58 1/2", and top and bottom 40 1/2".

For the bottom border, cut twelve 5 1/2" x 5 1/2" squares.

✿ DIRECTIONS

SEW-AND-FLIP PIECING TECHNIQUE

This style of piecing—a combination of Log-Cabin piecing and crazy patch—has many possibilities. The directions below are for the basic technique. Individual instructions are given for the blocks.

1. Cut a foundation piece of fabric 1/2" larger than the finished block. Then cut a starting piece of design fabric. It can be a lop-sided triangle, square, hexagon, etc. The fabric should take on the shape of the design in the finished block. (Look closely at the various blocks in the photograph for ideas.) Place the piece in the center of the block, off to the side, or in a corner, depending on the desired outcome.

2. Lay the second piece of fabric right sides together to one side of the first fabric. Stitch the pieces together through all three layers. Flip the second piece over, finger press, and trim to the shape you desire.

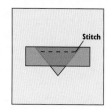
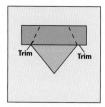

3. Continue this process until the foundation is full. As you work you can alter the shape of the piecing by how you trim.

4. If you want a particular shape to emerge, lightly sketch the shape on the muslin. Then as you add fabric to the center, you will see where you need to change color.

SUN, MOON, FLOWERS, AND FOLIAGE BLOCKS

Refer to Steps 1-4 of Sew-and-Flip Piecing. Interesting shapes emerge if you vary the color and placement of the first piece of fabric. As you compose the flower garden, create a transition from one block to the next by repeating a similar fabric along the edge where these blocks will be stitched together. When you view the composition, the seams will be less evident and the overall design is more dominant. Observe the piecing within the quilt to see how this was done.

SUNFLOWER BLOCK

1. Refer to Steps 1-4 of Sew-and-Flip Piecing. Sketch a simple sunflower on the foundation piece, making the petals large triangles.

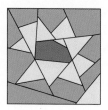

2. Place the first fabric close to the center of the foundation; it should be about 3" wide. Add the second strip and trim, as shown, to resemble a petal.

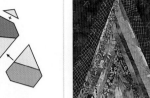

3. Stitch together a petal piece and a foliage piece and then add the second petal. Trim.

4. Continue adding sections as shown. After you have completed one sunflower, the second one will be easier. As you experiment with this technique you will realize that the piecing doesn't have to be exact. You are creating an impression.

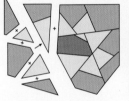

SUN BLOCK

Add the rays using the same method as for the sunflower petals. Notice that several fabrics are added around the first piece before the rays are added. Lightly sketching a design on muslin first will be helpful.

MOUNTAIN BLOCK

Add the rays using the same method as for the sunflower petals.

Notice that several fabrics are added around the first piece before the rays are added. Lightly sketching a design on muslin first will be helpful.

TREE BLOCKS

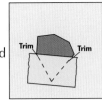

While the sun, moon, mountains, and flower blocks are sew-and-flip on a foundation of muslin, the trees are pieced blocks. Start with a triangle and continue piecing with strips until the block is 10 1/2" high. (The strips were cut 1" to 1 1/2" wide and the triangles were cut approximately 2 1/2" wide x 3" high.) Cut the pieces at random so that the trees will be different from each other. Once the strips have been added to make the trees 10 1/2" high, continue piecing strips on the sides until the blocks are at least 10 1/2" wide. Trim the blocks to 10 1/2" square. The scheme of "night and day" with the sun and moon repeats within the tree background.

✿ ASSEMBLY

1. Stitch together the flower and foliage blocks as shown, sewing the smaller blocks together first, then adding the larger ones. Press as you go.

2. Add the first border sides, then add the top and bottom borders. Press toward border. Repeat for the second border.

3. Assemble six tree blocks for the left side of the quilt and six for the right side. Join and add to the sides of the quilt. Press toward border.

---

4. Join the moon, mountains, and sun blocks, and add to the top of the quilt. Press toward border.

5. Arrange the twelve 5 1/2" squares for the bottom border and stitch together. Add to the bottom of the quilt. Press toward border.

✿ FINISHING

Refer to the Batting and Layering instructions on page 13. This was my very first attempt at free-motion machine quilting. I approached the quilting as if I were sketching, and kept in mind the details that I wanted to add in the different areas of the quilt. (I wanted the quilting to enhance and echo the pieced designs that I had created.) In some areas, I chose variegated threads to enhance the design. Refer to the Binding instructions on page 13.

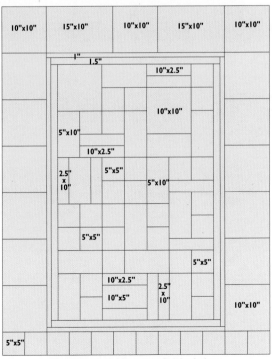

Measurements given are finished sizes.

FREDDY MORAN : Color Color Color!

Welcome to Freddy Moran's garden in Orinda, California. Freddy's home and her garden are entwined with their brilliant hues—as dynamic in color as her quilts. Large windows fill her house with light and call attention to the surrounding garden. Every room one sits in becomes part of the garden. Even near her sunny yellow quilting studio, where a stone wall outside the window might have been intrusive, roses emerge at the top—hot pinks, soft pinks, and purples radiate from the garden beyond. There is an excitement and adrenaline rush that comes with bright colors. For Freddy, this energy grows from putting colors together within her garden, which she then translates to her quilts. Freddy has an affinity for color that most of us do not, and you can feel this craving and pure enjoyment in all her work.

The process of gardening is what interests Freddy. If gardening weren't hands-on, Freddy claims she would not garden. Watering becomes the part of her daily routine in which she becomes intimately involved with the garden's welfare. "I go out early in the morning and I'm like a little pig squealing. I take off my shoes, hose down the patio wall while all is quiet, and see how all my little children did overnight. If I have sick babies I go around and check them. If I ever get to the point that I don't work with my hands in my garden, I think that there will be little joy left."

Freddy plants shade plants in the sun and full-sun plants in the shade—she likes to break all of the rules. There are too many rules in the world for Freddy, and she feels that people are afraid of breaking rules. This then becomes her challenge in gardening as well as quilting. Her mindset is evident in the colors she chooses and how she breaks the traditional rules of color theory. If someone tells her that she shouldn't put purple with yellow, she makes a point of doing so. Still, it is a great challenge for her to organize herself in the quilting process. Freddy always avoids the obvious and this is where her quilts become uniquely hers. If a design doesn't work, she retreats to her hammock in the garden and observes the garden, trying to figure out what makes "this and that" work.

When asked about the use of white in her garden, Freddy says that white sparks up the scene and makes the other colors lively. "White is a necessary beacon in a garden," she says, "especially when viewed at night. It lets the garden breathe. It is the same as working on a quilt and needing that relief from all the mediums and darks. I find I plan the color in my garden just as I plan my quilts. I never know the exact amount until the garden blooms and at that time I might move some of my white plants or add more. It's what feels like a pleasant balance."

The white in Freddy's garden pulls the eye from one direction to another. In her quilts, the black and white within the array of colors gives the eye a place to rest. It is her signature. Freddy might create a checkerboard or a picket fence or a simple band, but whatever the element, it pulls the composition together. There is a sense of fun in Freddy's quilt compositions that goes with her use of color.

Borders, whether in the garden or on a quilt, are Freddy's biggest stumbling block. But in both her garden and in quiltmaking, the borders are what Freddy does best! Usually they are complicated, intense, and interesting departures which pull the whole design together.

The connection for Freddy between gardening and quilting is the feeling of permanence. If you plant a tree you hope the tree will be there much longer than you are. The same is true with the quilts you sew. "I want to leave a heritage for my grandchildren," Freddy says. "I want them to know that I walked through this life and that I contributed. I think the same is true with the garden. The act of gardening and quilting, no matter how big or small, shows that you have really contributed. You have made a little corner of the world more beautiful. Everybody has to start somewhere. This is what I do."

Just Us Chickens

FREDDY MORAN

Quilted by Kathy Sandbach

56" x 63"

Chickens are the last thing you'd expect to find in this garden setting, but the image is typically "Freddy." I can always spot a quilt by Freddy at a show or in a book. She has a style all of her own. Her calling card is not only the whimsical play of elements in the quilt, but how she uses color. Her palette is vibrant and multi-faceted—all styles of fabrics come together to create a one-of-a-kind look.

Observe closely the styles and uses of the various fabrics in this quilt. Freddy puts stripes to good use to portray directional changes, right next to multicolored floral fabrics. The white picket fence has a calming effect on the formal part of this composition. Notice how she graduates the colors of the sky background fabrics within the tree blocks for the center of the quilt. A landscape rendered in perspective is created for the house to rest in. The choice of dark fabric for the house makes the block the center of attention.

❀ JUST US CHICKENS

❀ MATERIALS

This scrap-style quilt uses a variety of fabrics. General fabric amounts are given for each element. Look through your scraps or start collecting small cuts of a variety of fabric to reflect the palette you choose. Start the design at the center with the house block, then work toward the borders.

Assorted scrap fabrics:

- $1/3$ yard total of six fabrics for house
- $2/3$ yard for sky to appear with trees behind house and tall trees in top border
- $1/2$ yard of a bright green for yard
- $1/3$ yard of a light green for yard, house, and tree backgrounds
- $1/4$ yard for path
- $1/3$ yard for fence
- $3/4$ yard for short and tall tree tops
- $1/8$ yard each of two fabrics for tree trunks
- $1/2$ yard for short tree backgrounds
- $1/3$ yard for flower garden

First border: $1/8$ yard for top strip, $1/4$ yard for side and bottom strips

Chicken blocks:

- $1/4$ yard for chicken background
- $1/3$ yard for chicken bodies
- $1/8$ yard for beaks
- $1/8$ yard for combs
- $1/8$ yard for feet

- 1 yard for chicken borders and sashing, ground behind top row of trees, strip above top row of trees, and binding
- 1 yard for final border
- $3 1/2$ yards for backing
- 60" x 67" batting
- Template patterns, pages 124-125

❀ CUTTING

HOUSE BLOCK

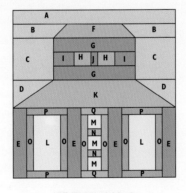

12" Finished block

A: cut one $1 1/2$" x $12 1/2$"

B: fold fabric right sides together, then cut two using template **B**

C: cut two $3 1/2$" squares

D: fold fabric right sides together, then cut two using template **D**

E: cut four $1 1/2$" x $5 1/2$"

F and **K:** cut one using templates **F** and **K**

G: cut two $1 1/2$" x $6 1/2$"

H: cut two $1 1/2$" x $1 3/4$"

I: cut two $1 1/2$" x 2"

J: cut one 1" x $1 1/2$"

L: cut two $2 1/2$" x $4 1/2$"

M: cut three $1 1/2$" squares

N: cut two 1" x $1 1/2$"

O: cut six 1" x $4 1/2$"

P: cut four 1" x $3 1/2$"

Q: cut two 1" x $2 1/2$"

FRONT YARD :

GRASS

Bright green: cut two $3 1/2$" x $10 1/2$" for yard; eight of piece **A** ($2 1/2$" x 3") for under the short trees; six $1 1/2$" x 40" strips to go between the fence rails.

Light green: for short trees, cut eight of piece **A** ($2 1/2$" x 3"), four pairs of piece **D** (fold fabric and cut using template **D**), and a $3 1/2$" x $24 1/2$" strip to go between the trees and house blocks.

PATH

Cut one $3 1/2$" x $4 1/2$" for upper path and one $4 1/2$" x $4 1/2$" for lower path between the fence.

FENCE

Cut five $1 1/2$" x 40" strips, then cut into thirty-four $4 1/2$" sections. Cut four 1" x 40" strips.

SHORT TREE BLOCK

6" Finished block

(Refer to the grass section above for cutting the pieces under the trees around the house). For the remaining trees, cut twenty-four of piece **A** (2 1/2" x 3"), twenty tree trunks of piece **B** (1 1/2" x 2 1/2"), and twenty tree tops using template **C**. For piece **D**, fold fabric right sides together and cut sixteen pairs (four of these are of sky fabric). Refer to the photograph as a guide.

GARDEN

A long strip is made for the garden, then the sections for the sides are cut off and pieced onto the side fences. Cut thirty-two 2 3/8" floral fabric squares. Cut sixteen 2 3/4" foliage fabric squares on the diagonal.

INNER BORDERS

First border: cut three 2 1/2" x 40" strips, then cut a 32 1/2" strip for the bottom, and two 36 1/2" strips for the sides.
Top border: cut a strip 2 1/2" x 32 1/2" from a different fabric than the first border fabric.

TALL TREE BLOCK

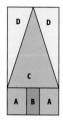

8" x 4" Finished block

A: cut two 2 1/2" x 2" each for twelve trees (total 24)
B: cut twelve 1 1/2" x 2 1/2"
C: cut twenty-four using template **C**
D: cut two each for twelve trees, fold fabric and use template **D**.

CHICKEN BLOCK

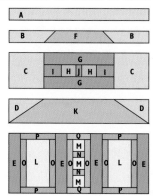

8" x 4" Finished block

Although there are nine total, cutting instructions are for only one block, so you can mix up the fabrics for each.

Background:
A: cut two 1 1/2" x 5 1/2"
B: cut 1 1/2" x 2 1/2"
C, **D**, and **G**: cut four 1 7/8" squares, then cut diagonally.
E and **H**: cut two 1 1/2" squares
Comb:
D: cut two 1 7/8" squares, then cut diagonally.
Beak:
G: cut one 1 7/8" square, then cut diagonally.
Feet:
C: cut one 1 7/8" square, then cut diagonally.
Body:
I: cut one 2 1/2" x 4 1/2"
F: cut one 2 1/2" square
Sashing:
• Cut two strips 1 1/2" x 40", then cut into eight 8 1/2" rectangles.
Stripe Border:
• Cut two 2 1/2" x 10 1/2" strips for the side borders of chickens.
• Cut four strips 1 1/2" x 40", then stitch together lengthwise. Cut two 44 1/2" lengths for the top and bottom borders of chickens. Cut one 48 1/2" length for border above the tall trees.

FINAL BORDER

Cut six strips 4 1/2" x 40", then stitch together lengthwise. Cut two 48 1/2" lengths for the top and bottom, and two 63 1/2" lengths for the sides.

✿ DIRECTIONS

1. Construct the house in rows.

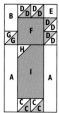

Stitch **B** to each side of **F**.
Stitch **I** to **H** to **J** to **H** to **I**, add **G** to the top and bottom, and add **C** to each side.
Stitch **D** to each side of **K**.
Stitch **O** to each side of **L**, add **P** to the top and bottom. Repeat.
Stitch **M** to **N** to **M** to **N** to **M**, add **O** to each side and **Q** to top and bottom.
Press the individual units.
Stitch **E** to a window to **E** to the door to **E** to a window to **E**. Press.
Join the rows together. Press.

2. The tree blocks, both short and tall, are all constructed in the same way. Stitch **D** to each side of **C**. Stitch an **A** to each side of **B**. Press. Join the two units. Press. Stitch six short trees together for each side. Stitch twelve tall trees together for the top border. Press.

  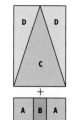

3. The fence is made of strips. For the fence rails, stitch grass and fence strips as shown. Press toward the grass.

Cut across the strips at 1 1/2" intervals. You'll need 34. Arrange the fence post strips and rail strips, as shown in the illustration, for the sides and front. Stitch together. Press. Freddy works very freely. These instructions will result in a slightly different fence than the one pictured.

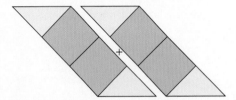

Cut into 1 1/2" intervals

4. Arrange the garden squares and half-square triangles. Stitch together in diagonal rows. Press. Cut two 8 1/2" lengths for sides and one 24 1/2" length for the bottom below the front fence.

5. Lay out the house block with yard and path. Stitch two short tree blocks together for each side, then join to the house. Press. Stitch yard rectangles to each side of the upper path, and add this section to the bottom of house. Press. Add strip of lawn to top of house. Press. Stitch four short tree blocks together and add to the top. Press.

6. Stitch a fence section to each side of the lower path. Press. Add to the bottom of the house block unit, press, then add the 24 1/2" garden section. Press. Stitch a fence section to the 8 1/2" garden strip. Press. Repeat for other side. Add the fence and garden units to each side. Press. Add first border to the top and bottom, then add to the sides. Press. Add the short tree borders to each side. Press.

7. Stitch the 1 1/2" x 48 1/2" stripe border to the top of the row of tall trees. Press. Join the tree row to the top of the house block unit. Press.

8. Lay out the pieces for one chicken block. Stitch the half-square triangle units together first (**G**, **D**, and **C**). Fold one of the 1 1/2" squares (**H**) of background fabric diagonally, and press. Unfold and place piece on the top left-hand corner of **G**. Stitch on the fold line. Trim off seam allowance. For the top and side combs, stitch two **D** units together. Stitch the two **C** units together for the feet. Join the pieces together in vertical rows. Press. Join the rows together. Press.

9. Stitch sashing between each of the chicken blocks, then add the top and bottom borders, then add the sides. Add to the bottom of the quilt. Press.

10. Add top and bottom of final border, then add sides. Press.

❀ FINISHING

Refer to the Batting and Layering instructions on page 13. Kathy Sandbach machine quilted the whimsical designs using variegated thread. "Just Us Chickens" is quilted in the side border (next to the chickens) and "Freddy Moran" is quilted at the bottom. You will find a hammock stitched in the lawn, feathers on the chickens, a curly flowering vine in the flowers, and clouds in the sky. The quilting is just as fun as the fabrics, color, and design of this quilt. Refer to the Binding instructions on page 13.

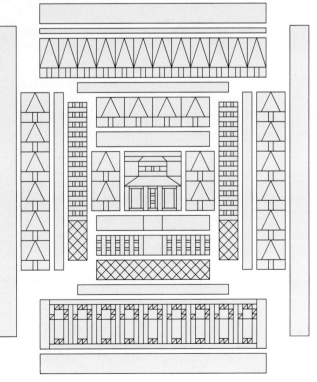

GWEN MARSTON: Mother Nature's Helper

When Gwen Marston first moved to her five acres on Beaver Island, Michigan, there was no house. The land in its natural state was so beautiful that Gwen was determined to change it as little as possible. Gwen sees herself as being a "land manager" for this informal landscape with four acres of hard woods, rather than a gardener.

Gwen's "garden" includes the ferns that make their home along the hillside, as well as the violets, bloodroot, wood lilies, wild daisies, knapweed, star flowers, pearly everlasting, and Indian pipe that have become part of the forest.

When choosing which flowers to plant, Gwen selects old-fashioned varieties. However, these must be hardy and grow in sandy soil. In the early spring hundreds of daffodils, red tulips, grape hyacinths, and crocus dot the landscape.

Every year for the past decade, Gwen has planted daffodils, which now number around six hundred. The daffodils are reliable and perform the best of all in the northern Michigan woods. They multiply every year and have naturalized in the woods and hillside around the house.

Early experiences often make dramatic impressions and influence people's lives. When Gwen was barely old enough to write her name, a book was given to her entitled, *The Magic Hill*, by A.A. Milne. The story is of a little princess who was named Daffodil by a good fairy. The fairy waved her magic wand and said:

"Let Daffodil the gardens fill.
Wherever you go flowers shall grow.
Thereafter with every step she took,
a flower grew as she lifted her little royal foot."

According to Gwen, "When I was little I remember so often looking over my shoulder to see if maybe, just maybe, a flower had sprung from beneath my heel." From visiting Gwen in her magical setting, one can see that her hand has enhanced the natural landscape and daffodils have sprung from her heel.

Now the daffodils are accented by bloodroot, with its tiny white flowers and big lacy leaves. Black-eyed Susans are scattered about. Native wood lilies find their way into the landscape all by themselves, while Gwen reminds the meadow roses that they can't just grow everywhere. In front of the house the field turns white with wild daisies, then purple with knapweed by spring's end. Both flowers make long-lasting bouquets to enjoy indoors.

An abundance of coreopsis supplies Gwen with yellow flowers for the summer. By mid-summer the air is sweet with the scent of milkweed, which invites swarms of Monarch butterflies. Last summer an amazingly tidy row of mullein appeared close to the screened porch. (This was one of Mother Nature's ideas.) The thick woolly leaves and long spikes of yellow flowers of these plants make them quite impressive. Gwen encourages volunteers by harvesting seeds and sprinkling them in other places on her five acres. Landscaping with hand-picked rocks and a wide variety of low ground covers make care and maintenance easy.

Fifteen-year old Pierson is Gwen's garden dog and faithful companion. Gwen plants extra daffodils every year since Pierson is known to roll in the flowers. He was born and raised on Beaver Island, and if you see Gwen, you'll see Pierson.

This quilter especially enjoys plants
from friends. Special friend Mary
Schafer sends gifts of candy tuft, iris,
lambs ear, pachysandra, and ajuga.
Mary taught Gwen how to hand
quilt many years ago and this lesson
paid off well: Gwen has written
numerous books on patchwork,
appliqué, and quilting. Mary's plants
have a special place in the landscape and remind Gwen of friend-
ships in quilting and gardening.

Daffodils in Spring

GWEN MARSTON
33 ¹/₂" x 30 ¹/₂"

It was only natural for Gwen to create an appliqué quilt of daffodils for this book. The minimal appliqué shapes used in the quilt lend themselves well to the folk-art appeal of Gwen's work. The petals are cut from three different yellow fabrics, and then arranged so the daffodils appear at different angles. The subtle change between the blue background fabric and the first border, with the addition of mini floral corner squares, is a nice touch.

Gwen chose printed crocus fabric for the border to keep the daffodils company, just as these flowers would in a spring garden. You could easily expand on this simple idea to create an even larger quilt with assorted blooms.

❀ DAFFODILS IN SPRING

❀ MATERIALS

- $5/8$ yard for center background
- $1/4$ yard for first border
- $1/8$ yard for corner posts of first border
- $1/4$ yard of two fabrics for second border and daffodils
- $1/8$ yard for daffodils and corner posts of second border
- $1/8$ yard for daffodil centers
- three 5" squares for birds
- $1/2$ yard for stems and leaves
- $1/2$ yard for third border
- $1/4$ yard for binding
- 1 yard backing
- 37" x 34" batting
- Template patterns on pages 123, 126-127

❀ CUTTING

Refer to the quilt for fabric placement. Cut center background fabric 20 $1/2$" x 17 $1/2$". For the first border, cut two sides 2 $3/4$" x 17 $1/2$", and the top and bottom 2 $3/4$" x 20 $1/2$". Cut four 2 $3/4$" square corner posts. For the second border, cut two sides 2" x 22" from one yellow fabric, and the top and bottom 2" x 25" from a second yellow fabric. Cut four 2" square corner posts from a third yellow fabric. For the third border cut two strips 3 $1/2$" x 28" for the top and bottom and two strips 3 $1/2$" x 31" for the sides.

Make a template for each appliqué shape. Trace around each template on the appropriate fabric. The number needed of each shape is written on the pattern. Add $1/4$" seam allowance around each shape before you cut them out.

❀ DIRECTIONS

Gwen used the needle-turn method to appliqué the top of this quilt. With this method, the appliqué shapes are cut out a scant $1/4$" larger than the pattern, then turned free hand with the needle as each is stitched. If you are more comfortable with the freezer-paper method, refer to pages 77-78 for instructions.

1. Stitch the sides of the first border to the center rectangle. Add the corner posts to each end of the top and bottom border strips, then add to the quilt. Press.

2. Position the appliqué shapes on the quilt top. Baste shapes in place with needle and thread through the middle of each shape.

3. To needle-turn appliqué, use the point of the needle to turn under the raw edge about $1/2$" at a time. Start by bringing the needle up from the back of the fabric through the folded-under edge of the appliqué and catch one or two threads. Bring the needle directly down through the background fabric to the wrong side of the top. Repeat the stitches about $1/8$" apart. Match the color of thread to appliqué fabric so very few stitches will show on the front of the quilt.

4. When necessary, clip a few threads into an inside curve, as was done for the bird shape.

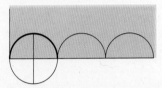
Clip

As you come to the end of a narrow leaf or point of a petal, turn under the point first, then turn the sides and work the raw edges under with the needle.

5. Add the second border, using the same sew order as in Step 1. Press.

6. For the final border add the top and bottom strips first, then add the sides. Press.

❀ FINISHING

Use the "tea cup" shape on page 123 to quilt the center section of the quilt.

Center the circle over the bottom of your quilt and trace around the top curve.

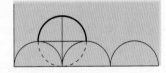

Continue making circles across the quilt. To begin making the second row, place the horizontal line on the tops of the first row of circles with the vertical line between the bottom two curves, and trace.

Refer to the Batting and Layering instructions on page 13. Double diagonal lines are quilted one inch apart through the second and third borders. Gwen whimsically put a dandelion fabric on the back of the quilt, hoping that there would be dandelions forever. Refer to the Binding instructions on page 13.

CATHERINE BRYAN: Country Spirit

Very "country and free spirited" best describes the garden and Catherine's own quilts, which reflect her casual Central Oregon lifestyle. Catherine and her husband built their magnificent log home on 80 acres and have developed the grounds with the native landscape in mind. Wildflowers are the mainstay; the medley changes from year to year depending on what re-seeds itself. Herbs grow in their own special bed right outside the kitchen window, where they are handy for cutting. Sunflower seeds are sown in the spring and bloom in the August sun. After the first frost, all of the remaining vegetable plants and herbs are cut back, along with the wildflowers around the pond.

Inside the home, threaded needles are lined up on the arm of the sofa, a fire is built in the fireplace, and quilt projects are started. Catherine hand quilts beside the fire and dreams of future quilts and gardens. She studies her notes on the different micro-climates that she's documented in her garden diary. Plans for spring are made, then seeds are ordered from catalogues.

Throughout the winter, Catherine's tea-colored log walls serve as a "design wall" where she works on quilts. Catherine's recognizable style comes out in her quilts, and a red or a shade of red is usually combined with vanilla cream, smoky gray, sage green, or pine tones. This color palette is evident in *Vanilla Rose*, showcasing a magnificent bouquet of roses.

Catherine Bryan and Edie Anniker-Hines are co-workers at The Stitchin' Post in Sisters, Oregon, and both women are avid quilters and gardeners. So it was only natural that when Edie announced her engagement, Catherine would offer to have the wedding in her garden. The garden view offers a scenic mix of wildflowers surrounding a pond, with nine snow-capped mountains.

As guests arrived for the wedding, children took rides in the canoe with Mel Bryan at the helm. Lotnig, Edie's horse, arrived all brushed and curried for the celebration. Wedding rings were tied in her mane and one of Edie's quilts was thrown over her back. As the celebration progressed wispy white clouds floated through a bright blue sky. Lavender pincushion flowers, yellow daisies, and baby's breath were picked early in the day and arranged casually in Catherine's collection of watering cans and buckets, which were then placed on the yellow checked tablecloths in the yard.

All of the employees at the store got into the act and contributed their quilts from the 1930's for the occasion. A special double wedding ring quilt in lavender, yellow, and green, belonging to Jean Wells, graced the bride and groom's table. The textured white wedding cake was decorated with simple Johnny Jump Ups in deeper purples and yellows. It was a beautiful day and a beautiful occasion.

Vanilla Rose

CATHERINE BRYAN

Quilted by Sue Nickels

92" x 104 3/4"

Each month at the Stitchin' Post one employee gets to have the others make a Double Nine-Patch quilt for them. When it was her turn, Catherine chose a garden theme using roses as her focus. (You can almost smell the lovely roses in this bouquet, which features *broderie perse* appliqué as well as piecing.) Once everyone was ready with the Nine-Patch blocks, Catherine started playing with the combinations on her design wall. She created a watercolor-style quilt with a traditional design. The lighter, more vanilla tones with soft, lighter pinks were used around the edges and the deeper tones in the center. A fabulous vintage rose fabric appeared in some of the companion blocks and was used for the appliqués. This helps to diminish the feeling of lines from the piecing and creates smoother, curvy lines that better represent the roses and leaves.

Catherine's signature plaid appears in the Nine-Patch blocks and again in the first border. Her work and her fabric choices radiate a Ralph Lauren mood, as does the decorating in her home.

INSTRUCTIONS
❀ VANILLA ROSE

❀ MATERIALS

As you select fabrics for the Nine-Patch blocks, be mindful of the "mood" of the bouquet, as you choose light, medium, and dark values. The low contrast of the companion squares creates a soft focus—the "vanilla"—with a few higher-contrast blocks in the middle of the bouquet. Look at the quilt, and proportion the fabrics into a group of 50% low contrast, 25% medium contrast, and 25% high contrast blocks. Catherine used a single fabric in the vase section and reversed it to create two color values.

- 2 1/2 yards each of mediums and darks, 2 yards of lights for Nine-Patches to appear in the body of quilt and border
- 1 1/2 yards of light, medium, and darks for companion squares
- 5 1/2 yards mixed light, medium, and dark fabric, with one fabric being a large floral for alternate blocks, quarter-square triangles, setting half-square triangles, and the appliqué
- 1/2 yard for the first border

- 2 1/2 yards for the second border, final border, setting triangles, and binding
- 8 yards for backing
- 96" x 109" batting

❀ CUTTING

Determine color and fabric placement before cutting fabrics or, cut the fabric for the Nine Patches first, construct the blocks, then cut the alternate and companion blocks as you build the design. The totals for each are given below.

Nine-Patches (294): Cut the Nine-Patch fabric into 1 1/2" strips.
Companion squares (164) for Double Nine-Patches: Cut 3 1/2" squares.
Alternate blocks (11): Cut 9 1/2" squares
Quarter-square triangles (72): Cut eighteen 14" squares, then diagonally in both directions.
Setting half-square triangles (46): Cut twenty-three 7 1/4" squares, then cut diagonally.
Vase half-square triangles (2): Cut one 10 7/8" square, then cut diagonally.

First border: Cut nine 1 1/2" strips.
Second border: Cut nine 2 3/4" strips.
Final border: Cut six 5 1/2" strips, then cut forty 5 1/2" squares. Cut these squares diagonally in both directions to have four setting triangles from each square. Border corner squares: Cut one 7" strip, then cut four 7" squares.

❀ DIRECTIONS

I. Make 294 Nine-Patch blocks, which also includes the block total for the vase and border. Note the color combinations—some are low contrast and some are high contrast. Unit 1 consists of a dark/light/dark combination. Stitch these together and press toward the dark strips. Unit 2 consists of light/dark/light combination. Stitch together, pressing toward the dark strip.

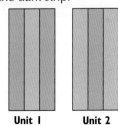

Unit I   Unit 2

2. Cut across the strips at 1 1/2" intervals.

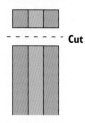

– – – – – – – **Cut**

3. Arrange the units as shown. To construct the block, place right sides together of row 1 to row 2, and stitch. Then add row 3. Press.

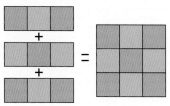

4. Once the Nine-Patches are finished, it's time to move to the design wall and start arranging the bouquet of flowers. Stitch the Double Nine-Patch blocks together first. (Stitch them as you did the single Nine-Patch blocks.) Press.

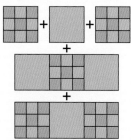

Double Nine-Patch, 9" Finished block

5. Stitch quarter-square triangle blocks together. See the quilt for fabric combinations. Press.

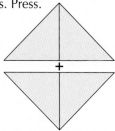

Quarter-square triangle block, 9" Finished block

6. Stitch the blocks together in a diagonal set. Press. Join row 1 to 2, etc. When you get to the bottom rows there will be a gap in the piecing where the vase will be appliquéd. Leave the gap open for now.

7. Press the quilt. Construct the vase, as shown. Note that the top half-square triangle is slightly larger. The other half, which you can trim later, will fit below. Stitch a line a scant 1/4" from the edge of the vase. Press under the seam allowances along this line on the sides and top. Pin to the quilt. Follow the appliqué instructions on page 49 and appliqué the vase to the quilt.

8. Trim the excess fabric underneath the vase to within 1/4".

9. Cut flower and foliage shapes, allowing for a 1/4" seam allowance. Position shapes on the quilt. Needle-turn appliqué in place. Note how Catherine has placed many over seams.

10. Stitch the first border strips together lengthwise. Press. Cut top and bottom 77". Stitch to quilt. Press. Cut sides 91 3/4". Stitch to quilt. Press.

11. Stitch second border strips together lengthwise. Press. Cut top and bottom 79". Cut sides 91 3/4". Set aside these second border strips until the final border is sewn together.

12. For the final border, Catherine set the Nine-Patches on point. Stitch a quarter-square triangle to each side of a Nine-Patch. Press. Stitch these together. Follow the illustration and make one long border strip. Press.

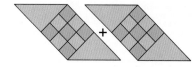

Cut final border strip top and bottom 79", sides 91 3/4", and trim the Nine-Patches as needed. Stitch second border strips to final border strips. Add corner squares to each end of the side border. Press.

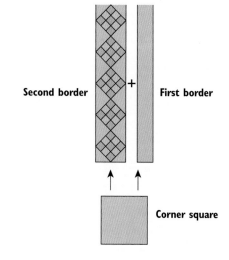

Second border   **First border**

Corner square

13. Add the top and bottom borders to the quilt, then add the sides to complete the quilt. Press.

❀ FINISHING

Refer to the Batting and Layering instructions on page 13. Curved feathers resembling growing plants are quilted in some of the Double Nine-Patches. Stipple quilting is used in the areas where there is less piecing. The over-all effect is of a sculptured vase of roses. Refer to the Binding instructions on page 13.

MARGARET PETERS:
Americana Collector

Margaret Peters is well-known within the quilt world for her collection of Americana and her love of America. The large flag hanging on her fence was a piece of corrugated metal roof that Margaret painted as a flag. Red, white, and blue memorabilia spill into the garden from her house. Flags, hand-painted signs of "Wing Town U.S.A." and "Rent for a Song", and many birdhouses form part of the display. Since bird-watching is a favorite pastime for the Peters, you will find little houses in unexpected places around the yard. A six-foot Uncle Sam stands guard over all the feeders. The memorabilia becomes more prominent in the winter months, when the yard is dormant, but year round the collection adds a touch of whimsy and color, and brings smiles to Pete and Margaret's faces—especially when the wind blows and the whirly-gigs are whirling in full force.

The Peters have one of the old farm houses in Walnut Creek, California. A large orchard of walnut and fruit trees are still a part of the yard. Through the years Margaret and Pete have planted hydrangeas, azaleas, and rhododendrons, and added a Fairy Jasmine under their bedroom window. A large redwood tree grows at the entrance to their driveway. Tiny potted plants and an assortment of other memorabilia greet visitors at the door. What pleasure this miniature garden setting gives everyone who knocks at the door.

Pete, a retired NFL football player, has a garden plot all his own. He always parks his 1955 red Ford truck beside an old gas pump in the front yard. However, several years ago he discovered that when he dumped the used pumpkins from Halloween in the yard next to the truck, the pumpkins grew vines and produced the next year! Now he plants his pumpkin patch even though the plants have taken over the entire area—climbing onto everything in sight, including his prize truck and the antique pump. Standing tall over the pumpkins are his twelve-foot sunflowers with blossoms over a foot across. Whatever is in the soil, the pumpkins and sunflowers love it!

Gardening and flowers have had a great influence on Margaret. By evidence of her quilts, it is no surprise that fall is her favorite season and chrysanthemums are her favorite flower. Margaret remarks that the leaves go out in a blaze of color and glory—telling us they will be back again—and sure enough the daffodils start the spring with their bright heads held under the new green leaves of those same trees. "Color is what we can learn from nature," adds Margaret. "The unexpected is always exciting and should be in your quilts." Look to the garden and find the "kicker" color: a color in a spot it was not intended, perhaps even a flower planted by the birds.

Uncle Sam Lives Here

MARGARET PETERS
33" x 26"

Margaret re-created her own backyard in appliqué with a collage-style technique. Bits and pieces of fabrics, carefully chosen to resemble the actual setting, were fused in place and then buttonhole stitched by machine. According to Margaret, you shouldn't hesitate to create your own backyard or make that fabulous "yard of your dreams" using this technique.

To start, take pictures of your yard then enlarge the image on a photocopier and you will magically have your pattern. When looking for fabric, remember you are only using small pieces, so a portion of a large print may be all that you need. Look at the fabric for its textural quality. A basket texture may come from a floral print. Add details with embroidery stitches, as Margaret did for the wisteria or the tiny yoyos made for the hollyhocks.

Play with your fabric and see what you can invent. Once Margaret needed autumn leaves one-half inch or less, but all she had were leaves two to three inches—until she told herself the fabric doesn't know what size the leaves are. Margaret drew the size of leaf she needed and it worked. Overlap several pieces to make a statement. Some of the garden plants spill over the planters and pots, and Margaret mimics this by making small cuts into the flower groups so they can drape over a pot or basket.

❀ UNCLE SAM LIVES HERE

❀ MATERIALS

- 1 yard muslin
- $1/4$ yard sky print fabric
- $3/8$ yard wood print for fence
- $1/4$ yard grass print
- $1/4$ yard brick or gravel print for path
- $1/8$ yard rock print for wall
- 3 different wood print scraps for the chair and tree trunks (the large tree is 18" x 18")
- Various scraps of flowers and two or three shrub print fabrics
- Scraps for Uncle Sam, bird bath, bird houses, black for plant hanger and birds, brown for squirrels, terra cotta or gray for bird bath, blue water, brown for bunny, green for hollyhock leaves
- Theme fabrics such as pails, shovels, seed packets, gardening hat, gloves, wheel barrow, etc.
- $1 1/2$ yards for border, binding, and backing
- 1 skein six-strand variegated lavender or purple floss for wisteria
- 1 skein six-strand variegated rose floss for hollyhocks
- 1 skein #3 or #5 perle cotton for hollyhock stem
- 1 skein six-strand black floss if stitching appliqués by hand or try Jean's Stitch™ Thread or machine embroidery thread if buttonhole stitching by machine
- Black permanent fine point pen for drawing Uncle Sam's face, the flag pole, and other details
- 3 yards paper-backed adhesive
- 37" x 30" batting
- Appliqué patterns on pages 128-130

❀ CUTTING

Cut muslin 21 $1/2$" x 28 $1/2$".

Cut sky fabric and paper-backed adhesive 8" x 28 $1/2$"

Cut fence fabric and paper-backed adhesive 9 $1/4$" x 28 $1/2$"

Cut grass fabric and paper-backed adhesive 5 $1/4$" x 28 $1/2$"

Cut four 3" x 40" border strips. Trim sides to 21 $1/2$", and the top and bottom to 33 $1/2$".

❀ DIRECTIONS

Margaret likes to work on a flat surface, such as an old table-top with a towel spread over it, so she doesn't have to lift up the project and transport it to the ironing board as she fuses the shapes. But this method only works on with laminated surfaces. Don't use your good dining-room table because when you press with the iron, the towel might stick to the wood finish.

1. Trace all of the appliqué shapes on the paper side of the paper-backed adhesive. A dotted line means one piece overlaps another. Place the paper appliqués on the wrong side of their appropriate fabric. Fuse in place following the manufacturer's instructions. Cut the shapes. Also fuse paper-backed adhesive to various flower, shrub, and theme fabrics. Cut out the desired shapes.

Tip: If you have trouble peeling the paper from the appliqué, try this technique from Margaret. Take a straight pin and simply score the back of the paper. Bend along the scoring and peel the paper off.

2. First place the sky on the muslin, overlapping it slightly with the fence. Add some of the shrubs and flowers. Then add the grass and pathway. Fit the rocks and more shrubs and flowers along the fence line.

3. Place the various appliqués, working in layers from the fence. Add the major pieces first, then add the details. Once you are satisfied, fuse the shapes in place, following the manufacturer's instructions.

4. Buttonhole stitch by hand or machine. The directions for hand stitching are on pages 114-115. Embellish with embroidery floss, perle cotton, and permanent ink details.

5. Add the side borders, then the top and bottom. Press.

Tip: Margaret made tiny yo-yos for the hollyhock flowers. Cut 1 $1/8$" circles from the fabric using the pattern on page 130. Run a small gathering stitch $1/8$" from the outside edge. Pull the gathering thread tightly and secure the end, but do not cut off the thread. Flatten to form flowers, with the gathered side up. Attach yo-yos to the quilt through the gathered centers.

❀ FINISHING

Because the background is fused, it would be impossible to hand quilt this wallhanging. Instead, layer, pinbaste, and machine stitch around the major images. Then add a few detail lines within the design.

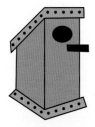
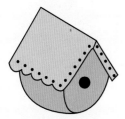

Bird houses

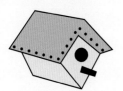

Flower pot

Water can

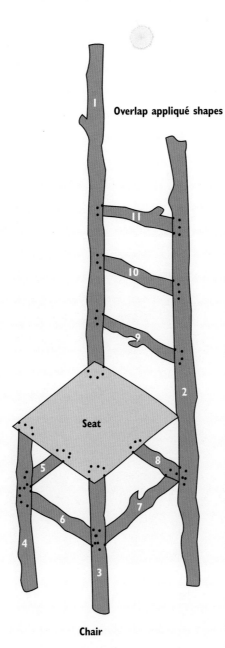

Overlap appliqué shapes

1
11
10
9
2
Seat
5
8
7
6
4
3

Chair

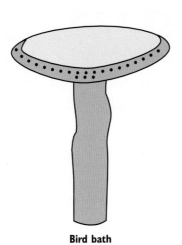

Bird bath

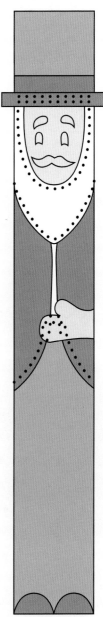

Uncle Sam

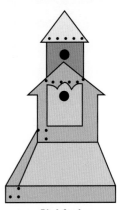

Bird feeder

TONYE PHILLIPS:
Quaint Cottage Garden
Nestled in the Mountains

S trolling toward Tonye's rustic home is like going back in time. The house is in a mountain meadow in the snow-capped Cascades, surrounded by pine and aspen trees. Although the winters are harsh and there is frost almost every month of the year, the setting is very tranquil.

The Phillips' casual lifestyle is reflected in their yard and garden. There is plenty of room for their children to run or to play in the creek which runs along the edge of the property. Although the front of the house is closed in with large ponderosa pines, the meadow area in the back of the house has been kept clear to enhance the open feeling. Tonye finds that in the summer it is especially nice to have shade in the front and sun in the back. Through trial and error Tonye has further improved the setting by creating an old-fashioned flower and vegetable cottage garden (complete with picket fence) to be envied by all.

As you stroll through the yard, a glimpse of a willow settee in a grove of aspens may catch your eye, or Tonye's blue bicycle from childhood resting against the fence, or the wreath made of hop vines hanging on the greenhouse to welcome you. These touches make visiting this quaint cottage garden a serene experience.

Tonye's husband, Doug, built a greenhouse from antique windows and a foundation of rocks gathered in the area. The greenhouse extends the growing season and makes it possible to grow more fragile plants. Miniature gardens planted in pots move in and out of the greenhouse at night as the evenings start to cool.

"Letting plants grow as they wish" is Tonye's motto. Her *Flower Power* quilt follows this philosophy. The fine hand quilting stitches of flower petals remind one of the flowers from the summer season. Simple vines quilted in the green sashing further portrays her garden. The actual quilting is Tonye's favorite part of creating a quilt. Her quilts are always based on fine hand-quilted designs, which become livelier as stitches are added to each block. Tonye loves working on muslin, and can hardly wait to wash the quilt. When washed, the quilt transforms from a "new" quilt to one with an antique look. These quilts have a nostalgic mood, as much as her garden does.

Planning is not at the top of Tonye's list of garden chores, although she does consider sun and shade when she plants. Over the years she's chosen the plants she likes: foxgloves, bleeding heart, sweet William, Jacob's ladder, poppies, and pansies, and placed them lovingly in her cottage garden. Her fondness for old-fashioned plants is very evident as you view the mixture of flowers and vegetables she grows. For the deck she creates potted gardens with the more fragile flowers like zinnias and nasturtiums.

Throughout the fall an oil lantern left on at night keeps the temperature above freezing and provides the family with fresh tomatoes and other garden treats.

Tonye's boys get into the gardening mood, too. They are encouraged to plant their own gardens within the greenhouse. Peas are a favorite plant to grow, but the most excitement comes from harvesting the vegetables. You will find them digging up carrots and potatoes for supper, or picking pea pods for a snack. Tonye remarks that this is a wonderful way to get them to eat their vegetables.

Love of gardening is deeply rooted in this woman. At parochial school, Tonye used to garden with the nuns. "Nurturing" is at the heart of Tonye's involvement in her home and garden. In gardening, Tonye considers "soil is everything." Springtime will find her dressing the beds and garden plot with organic compost. Tonye incorporates the compost into the soil by spading as close to the perennials as possible, then adding granule fish fertilizer. Through the season, she fertilizes with liquid fish fertilizer once a month. Her plants thrive in the well-nurtured environment. Bugs fend for themselves. If necessary, Tonye sprays with soapy water to control the insects.

As the fall season starts, ever too quickly for this family, it is time to put the garden to bed. The season's foliage is cut back and the perennials are nestled under a blanket of pine needles for the winter. Snow comes early to this part of Oregon, and the cold stays for several months.

As the snow begins to fall, the garden setting changes rapidly. Little white lights are strung in the greenhouse and across the trellis covered with dried hop vines. The lights sparkle in the snow creating a winter wonderland. On an overcast day the setting resembles a black and white photograph. The greenhouse glimmers from a blanket of white. The garden is at rest!

When all is said and done, Tonye enjoys the fruits of her labor and being able to share it with others, be it a bouquet of flowers or fresh vegetables, or a chat in the garden. Her joy is always looking forward with great anticipation to the next planting or the next quilt design.

Flower Power

TONYE PHILLIPS
55 1/2" x 66 1/2"

"Let your imagination run wild with this quilt" advises Tonye. That's just what she did. She started with free-form cut circles, two for each block, overlapping. The fabrics are wild and playful. As Tonye says, "the circles are a little goofy so I hope this sets the tone for the entire quilt." The real fun began for this prolific quilter, who hand quilts almost every day, when her imagination came into play. She penciled in the petal shapes, then stitched around the flower centers. Tonye marked the designs as she went to allow herself more time to dream as she quilted. All those years of gardening and observation paid off. Early on she asked her young sons, Charlie and Ande to choose their favorite blocks. She carefully sketched the letters of each name around a flower center. Then Doug, her husband, chose his block, and she added her name, Tonye Belinda, to her own favorite. Can't you just see someone finding this quilt a hundred years from now and trying to figure out what all this meant? Fortunately, Tonye has stitched a beautiful label for the back.

The dark gray-green fabric is perfect for the sashing and the quilted vine design. "Flower Power" is further repeated in the colored squares set on-point in the border. Tonye recommends not worrying if the border squares don't fit perfectly at the corners. If you have to chop them partially off, so be it! That is part of the charm of this type of quilt.

❀ FLOWER POWER

❀ MATERIALS
- 1 yard total of assorted scraps for the flower centers and small border squares.
- 1 3/4 yards good quality muslin for blocks and pieced diamond border
- 1/2 yard for narrow second and final borders
- 2 1/4 yards for sashing, corners, first border, and binding
- 3 1/3 yards backing
- 58" x 70" batting
- Assorted colors of quilting thread
- Plastic-coated freezer paper for appliqué

❀ CUTTING
Cut thirty-two 7" squares from the muslin. Cut sixteen 2" x 40" strips from the sashing fabric, then cut the strips into thirty-eight 7" lengths. Stitch the remaining strips together to make the long sashing pieces.

For the side triangles, cut four 10 1/2" squares, then cut these diagonally in both directions to give you four triangles from each square.

For the corners, cut two 7 3/4" squares, then cut these diagonally.

For the first border, cut six 2" x 40" strips. Stitch strips together lengthwise, then cut sides 59", and the top and bottom 50".

Cut twelve 1" x 40" strips for the narrow second and final borders. Stitch strips together lengthwise. For the second border cut sides 62", top and bottom 51". For the final border cut sides 66 1/2", top and bottom 55 1/2".

For the pieced diamond border, cut one-hundred thirty-six 1 3/4" squares from assorted scraps. There will be a few extras if you want to switch colors. Cut thirty-one 3" squares from muslin, then cut these in half diagonally in both directions.

❀ DIRECTIONS

Flower block

1. Randomly draw one large (3-4" diameter) and one smaller (1-3" diameter) circle on the non-coated side of the freezer paper. Cut out the circles and place the coated side of the paper on the wrong side of the fabric. Cut out the circles allowing about 1/4" seam allowance from the edge of the paper. Clip around the edges for easing.

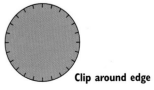

Clip around edge

2. Match the appliqué thread to the fabric so it doesn't show. Appliqué the larger circle first onto the muslin. Using the needle, push under the seam allowance of the appliqué an inch at a time. Using a single thread knotted at one end, bring the needle up along the edge of the appliqué coming through the muslin and taking a couple threads of the appliqué. Take the needle back to the wrong side of the block and come up a small stitch away, repeating the process. With this method, the bulk of the thread is carried on the wrong side of the block as the thread comes up to catch the appliqué, which gives a neat look to the appliqué.

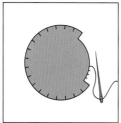

3. After the circle is stitched, slit the muslin behind the circle and pull out the paper. Trim muslin to within ¹/₄" of the appliqué line.

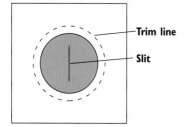

Trim line
Slit

4. Stitch the second circle on top of the first one, using the same method in Steps 2 and 3.

5. Arrange the blocks as you like. Insert the 7" sashing pieces between the blocks. Then add the side triangles and corners.

6. Stitch the triangles, blocks, and short sashing strips together in rows, in a diagonal set. Press. Measure the rows and cut seven long sashing strips to go between the rows. Join the rows to the long sashing pieces, then add corner triangles. Press.

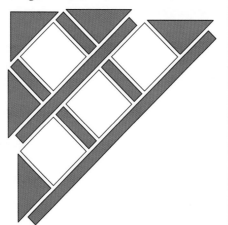

7. Add the first border, stitching the side strips first and then the top and bottom. Press. Repeat for the narrow second border.

8. For the diamond border, join all the squares and triangles as shown. Press.

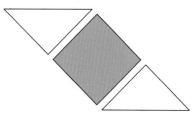

9. Cut the diamond side borders 63" and the top and bottom borders 54 ¹/₂", chopping off the diamond points as needed. Attach the side borders first, then add the top and bottom borders. Press.

10. Add the final border, stitching the side strips first, then the top and bottom. Press.

❁ FINISHING

Quilting patterns are provided for some of the petal shapes in the flowers and the vines. If you study flower shapes in your garden, or in seed catalogues, you will find even more ideas. The shapes are lightly penciled in, then stitched in colored thread. To make the letters for the names, put a piece of tracing paper over the flower center and write the name in a circle. This will give you an idea for spacing. Now add lines on each side of the letters to make them about 1/4" to 3/8" wide. Cut them out, spacing the letters around the block and tracing around them. Tonye used 1" grid quilting in the side triangles and the diamond border.

Quilt designs can be found on page 131. Enlarge the ones for use around the flower centers 200%.
Layer and baste (page 13), after marking the quilt top. Refer to the Binding instructions on page 13.

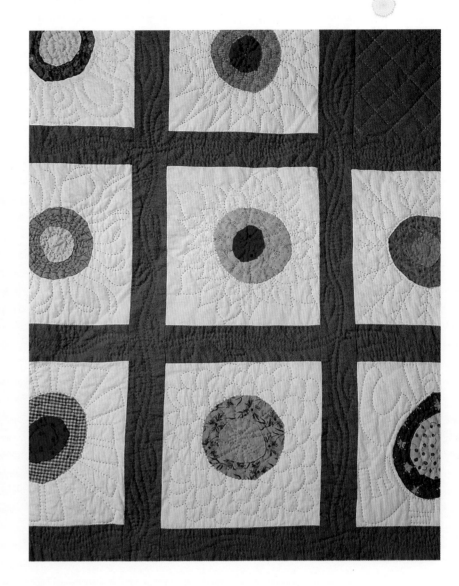

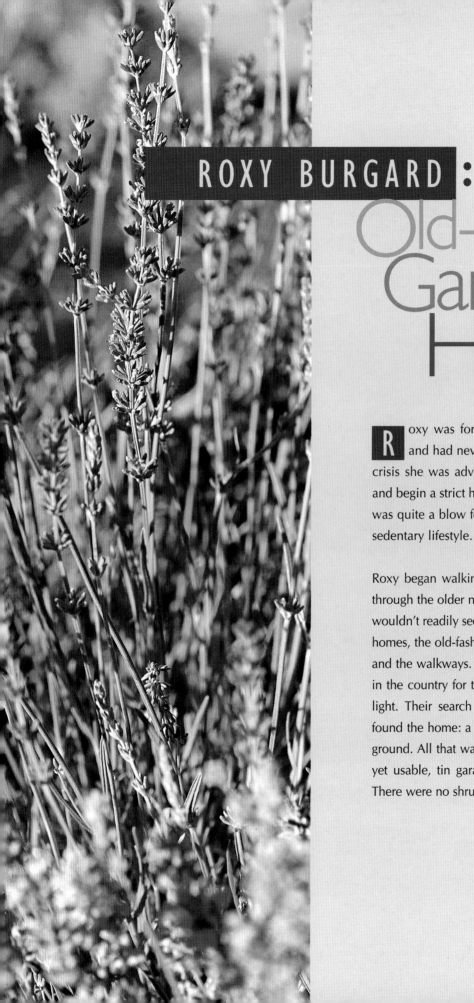

ROXY BURGARD:
Old-Fashioned Garden with History

Roxy was forty-four years old, out-of-shape, overweight, and had never spent much time outside. During a health crisis she was advised by her doctor to lose weight, exercise, and begin a strict healthy eating plan for the rest of her life. This was quite a blow for a quilter who liked cookies and had led a sedentary lifestyle.

Roxy began walking religiously four miles a day. Taking strolls through the older neighborhoods, she started noticing things one wouldn't readily see from a car: the character and charm of older homes, the old-fashioned perennials in the yards, the large trees, and the walkways. She and her husband, Dave, decided to look in the country for the house of their dreams; a home filled with light. Their search took them to only two listings before they found the home: a 1906 renovated farmhouse with two acres of ground. All that was left of the yard, however, was an unsightly, yet usable, tin garage and a 100-year-old English walnut tree. There were no shrubs or flowers of any kind.

Roxy began formulating ideas for the yard based on all the walks she had taken through the neighborhoods. Then she began to read and study gardening books. Five years later the land has been tamed, but the garden will never be done! Roxy's since acquired a "farmer's tan" (arms and neck only), her hands are permanently stained from the red soil, and she has gardener's knees and a back that goes out. But they've also hauled truck-loads of fill dirt, gravel, compost, and landscape rock, and the thistles have been replaced by white picket fences, climbing roses, rusty farm implements, hollyhocks, sweet peas, and cottage and herb gardens.

As you drive up the gravel road, thirty-five varieties of lavender greet you and an antique quilt, hung on the original farmhouse clothesline, flutters gently in the breeze. The scent of lavender embraces you, and one is reminded of days gone by and fresh linens in grandmother's closet.

"Quilting and gardening are my heart and soul!" proclaims Roxy. "To everything there is a season, and a time to every purpose under heaven…for me the seasons of my life revolve around gardening in the spring and summer (a time to sow) and quilting in the fall and winter (a time to sew). I think we are just visitors here for a short time and I want to leave something beautiful in the form of flowers and quilts when I am gone!" Roxy's legacy will truly be a bountiful garden and many beautiful quilts.

When I first met Roxy, she had a quilt shop called Thread Bear Studio. The store was filled with themes similar to those I see in her garden. Her wholesale pattern company, "Calico Hills Farm" carries quilts in the pattern line which not only reflect her love of gardening but also illustrate her love of antique quilts.

Roxy began her lavender patch innocently enough; she started with just two plants. However, her attraction to the gray-green foliage and the pretty lavender blooms, the wonderful fragrance, the plant form, its hardiness, and the old-fashioned charm gave her liberty to spend the long winter hours researching the history of the plant. Roxy found very little information available on the different varieties, so she decided to buy as many as she could find, and see what each was like. The differences in color, shape, and size are all amazing. As you can see they are all beautiful in their own special way.

In the garden, "things" have been added to the landscape to create themes. An old porch post stands tall in the corner of the garden with signs pointing to all of Roxy and Dave's favorite places. Pointing north is Starbucks Coffee® 6 miles, Whidby Island is 272 miles north, and east it's 112 miles to The Stitchin' Post in Sisters. These mementos make the garden very personal. Memorabilia tucked in among the plants speaks of Roxy's love of farms. In the "thyme" garden you will find an alarm clock and a sundial.

The cottage garden, first designed on graph paper (a habit learned from quilting), has the symmetry of an Amish quilt. Yet, when filled with vegetables, flowers, and memorabilia, this garden takes on a life all of its own. What tames the garden is the quilt layout, making the caretaking, weeding, and watering extremely easy. This garden tells you a great deal about Roxy and her love of gardening and quilting. The vision and attention to detail not only in the structure but also in the planning and nurturing make Roxy's garden a treasure for the senses.

Lavender Patch

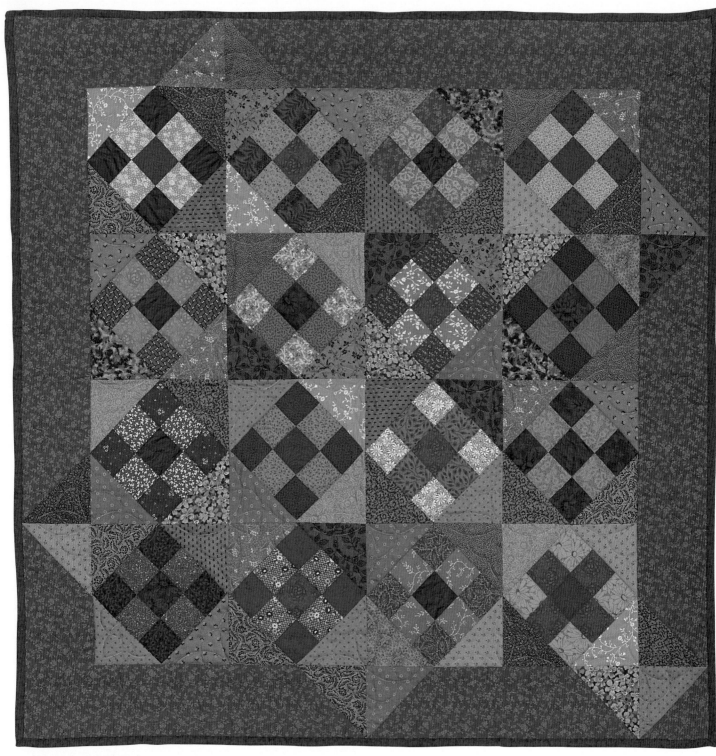

ROXY BURGARD

Quilted by Katrina Beverage

38" x 38"

The process of working on quilts, from dreaming, planning, and drafting, to buying supplies, cutting, stitching, and then quilting, is similar to gardening. So it is not surprising that Roxy chose a lavender theme for her Nine-Patch quilt. The simple patches set the tone in this old-fashioned quilt of soft gray-greens and a variety of lavenders. Like many quilters Roxy takes her color clues from experience and observation. "Mother Nature always knows her colors—green is always right with every other color and greens never clash! A yellow center always gives a spark and there are no 'original' color schemes...all color comes from nature!"

Roxy transforms a simple Nine-Patch on point into an elegant portrayal of a lavender garden with her choice of color and quilt block setting. Letting the green half-square triangles extend into the border, as foliage does in the garden, moves the gaze around, then in and out of the quilt.

❀ LAVENDER PATCH

❀ MATERIALS

- 1 1/3 yards total of thirty-six various lavenders and purples for Nine-Patch blocks
- 6" x 12" scraps of twenty-two various greens for triangles (consider increasing the amount of your favorite green and lavender fabrics)
- 7/8 yard medium-dark purple for border
- 1/4 yard for binding
- 1 1/8 yards for backing
- 42" x 42" batting

❀ CUTTING

NINE-PATCH BLOCK

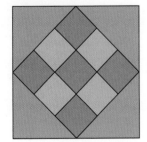

5 1/4" Finished block

Cut four 2 1/4" squares from each of the thirty-six lavender and purple fabrics (144 total).
Cut thirty-eight 4 5/8" squares from the twenty-two green fabrics, then cut the squares diagonally (75 total).

Border (all measurements listed are exact, cut the strips a little longer than needed)

B, H: two 4 1/4" x 30"
D: one 4 1/4" x 26"
F: one 4 1/4" x 22"
E: one 4 1/4" x 18"
A, C, G: three 4 1/4" x 15"
Triangle **I2:** 4 5/8" square, cut diagonally

❀ DIRECTIONS

NINE-PATCH "FLOWERS"

I. Choose sixteen 2 1/4" squares from the darkest fabric to use as the flower centers. Then pair up a "flower" fabric and a "corner" fabric for each flower. Lay out and group squares for sixteen blocks. Refer to the photograph for placement ideas.

2. Stitch the squares together in rows, then press. Stitch the rows together as shown, and press.

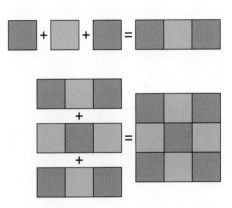

TRIANGLE "LEAVES"

I. Lay out the Nine-Patch blocks as you want them to appear in the quilt. Insert the green half-square triangle "leaves" within the layout. Reserve eleven triangle leaves for the border.

2. With right sides together, stitch the half-square triangles to the blocks, as shown. Press toward the half-square triangles.

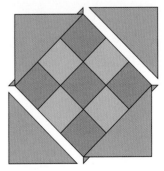

3. Square up blocks to 8", if needed.

JOINING BLOCKS

1. Lay out the blocks again as you want them to appear in the quilt. Stitch them together in rows, then join the rows as you did with the Nine-Patch block, and press.

BORDERS

1. Arrange triangle leaves and border pieces, as shown.

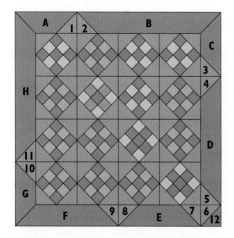

2. For each triangle, match a straight grain side, right sides together, with an appropriate end of a border strip, as shown. Stitch, then trim away excess border strip. Press.

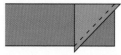

3. Use the same method as in Step 2 for adding all triangle "leaves" to border strips as follows:
Stitch triangle **1** to border **A**, then **2** to **B**, **3** to **C**, and **4** to **D**.
Do not stitch triangles **5**, **6**, and **7** yet.
Stitch triangle **8** to **E**, **9** to **F**, **10** to **G**, and **11** to **H**.

4. Stitch top borders **A** and **B** together. Stitch **C** and **D** together. Stitch **E** and **F** together. Then stitch **G** and **H** together. Press.

5. Piece together half-square triangles **6** and **12**, then press.

ADDING TRIANGLES 5 AND 7 TO BORDERS

Use the following method to mark exact placement of triangles onto the border.

1. Lay **CD** border along right side of quilt top, matching triangles **3** and **4** to their adjoining seam on the quilt.

2. Mark the exact spot with a pencil dot on the border strip's seamline where triangle **5** should be. Also mark the lower seamline corner on triangle **5**.

3. Place triangle **5** right sides together with border, using the same method as in Borders, Step 2. Pin and stitch, then trim excess border strip. Press seam toward triangle **5**.

4. Lay **EF** border along bottom edge of quilt top, matching triangles **8** and **9** to their adjoining seam on the quilt.

5. Place triangle **7** right sides together with border, using the same method as in Borders, Step 2. Pin and stitch, then trim away excess border strip. Press seam toward triangle **7**.

6. Join corner square **6/12** to **EF** border at triangle **7**, matching seams. Press.

7. Stitch **CD** side border to quilt, leaving mitered seam at upper right corner open (1/4" from cut edge) and matching seams of intersecting triangles. Press.

8. Stitch **EF** bottom border to quilt, leaving mitered seam at lower left open (1/4" from cut edge) and matching seams of intersecting triangles. Press.

9. Stitch **GH** border and **AB** border to quilt, matching seams of intersecting triangles and leaving diagonal mitered corner seams open (1/4" from cut edge). Press.

MITERED BORDERS

For the three corners that need mitering, the border seams should be stitched to within 1/4" of the corner.

1. Place the quilt, wrong side up, on your ironing board. Fold the corners of the strips down at an exact 45° angle from where the stitching stopped. Match both sides of the miter in each corner and press.

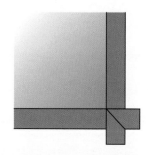

Wrong side of quilt

2. Take the quilt top to the sewing machine and with right sides of strips together and the quilt top folded out of the way, sew along the crease of the border only from the quilt top diagonally to the outside corner, backstitching at the beginning and end of the seam. Repeat for the other corner miters. Trim seam allowance to 1/4", then press the seam open.

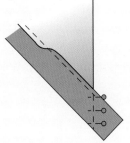

✿ FINISHING

Refer to the Batting and Layering instructions on page 13. A cable design was quilted in the border and a simple floral motif in the green triangle areas. Refer to the Binding instructions on page 13.

DENNIS McGREGOR: Backyard Garden

Dennis has been a gardener since he can remember. His mother was a landscape architect, his dad was born and raised on a farm, and his grandfather started one of the largest plant nurseries in Salt Lake City. Dennis always worked in the yard as a kid, and later, when he was at college, he and a friend got permission to turn a vacant lot on the campus into a vegetable garden. But it was not until he moved to Sisters, Oregon, that he—with the urging of his wife, Marcie—started working flowers into the vegetable garden setting.

Gardening is very therapeutic for this well-known artist who has chosen to live in the heart of downtown Sisters. Since he isn't one who likes to go to the gym, the physical exercise involved in gardening keeps him active while mentally and spiritually stimulating him. Evidence of this shows in the original art he created for the forest service, fish and wildlife service, the Sisters' rodeo, and the Sisters' quilt show.

Dennis likens the garden in the spring to a blank canvas. Placing the seeds is akin to sketching. The knowledge of plants—their height, width, and amount of sunshine they need—helps Dennis compose on this canvas of soil. When the garden is in full bloom the planning of the spring planting is evident in the layers of plants. Green beans are planted next to sunflowers to use their hardy stems for climbing. A row of zinnias are tightly packed in front and another row of marigolds in front of the zinnias.

As plants come up in the spring they are allowed to develop, then are often moved to a more pleasing place aesthetically, a place to better please the eye or have room to mature. Simplicity and common sense are evident here. A lone larkspur appears mystically in the middle of the peas, making it obvious that the garden has a mind of its own even with the planning that Dennis does.

Dennis explains that he found the garden plot when he and his family moved into Tillie Wilson's house. She was a school teacher in Sisters from the early 1900s until the 1950s and cultivated quite a plot. As Dennis and Marcie cleaned up the overgrown backyard they discovered many old trees, shrubs, and perennials, such as dogwood, lilac, hollyhocks, Virginia creeper, snowberry, Oregon grape, and climbing roses at the edge of the shed, along with marbles and tarnished silverware that probably came from Tillie's sons.

Dennis noticed the vegetation on a walk along the nearby Deschutes river, and it occurred to him that Tillie and her family had probably dug up plants from along the river, since these natives were so well represented in her yard and there weren't any plant nurseries in her time. Tillie had left a piece of the past in this setting, one to be discovered by the next home owner.

Being a composter, Dennis was thrilled to find a metal-lined hole dug into a corner of the garden. It is still in use and great pleasure comes from watching the birds peck at the vegetable material in the pile. The original wood shed has been left intact with hollyhocks, roses, bachelor buttons, and Virginia creeper along the edge just as Tillie intended, and is now used as a garden shed.

As a commercial artist, Dennis works on anything and everything. Once he became a neighbor of mine at The Stitchin' Post, we began talking about the possibility of his producing a painting that could be used to promote the quilt show. At the time he really didn't know much about quilts, but when faced with the assignment he began studying quilts intensely. He discovered that he liked what he saw. It was amazing to him to realize what pioneer women accomplished, while managing to create beautiful designs and patterns in their spare time. The scraps of old clothes that found their way into intricately pieced quilts made him aware that recycling is not new. He developed a strong sense of respect for these women and he feels that it is evident that every person, no matter what his or her means, has an innate ability to create something beautiful.

When you view the 1998 Sisters Outdoor Quilt Show painting that Dennis created, you are captured by the mix of vegetables and flowers in the setting of pine trees. You will see the same setting in his backyard. As Dennis began studying elements in the garden, the vegetable and flowers became the frame of reference that he used in the repeating quilt designs. Studying the light patterns at different times of day gave him inspiration for his paintings of the last seven years. He finds that traditional, geometric patterns translate better in painting rather than free-flowing contemporary designs. The strength of pattern is the focal point of his designs.

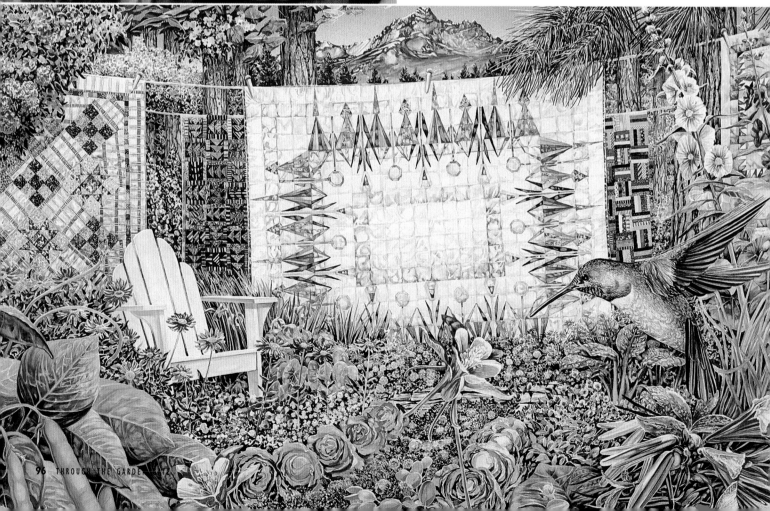

Gardens and quilts continue to inspire this artist and you will now find him working on a series of signed and numbered limited edition prints that will be available by mail. The first in the series pictured here was inspired by the wild yellow roses seen as a backdrop in his own backyard. Appliquéd spring and summer flowers serpentine over the quilt. Wouldn't it be fun to interpret the painted quilt in fabric?

McGregor's Garden

Designed by Dennis McGregor, made by Jean Wells and Jackie Erickson
Quilted by Katrina Beverage
80 1/2" x 96 1/2"

When Dennis finished the annual quilt show painting, I offered to make the quilt. It was easy to transform *McGregor's Garden* into a workable idea, using his sketches drawn on an orderly grid. Dennis spent several hours mulling over fabric choices and arrived at this palette, which is a good combination in fabric style. I found it very interesting to watch him make these choices and I learned from him as he interpreted the images into fabric.

Jackie Erickson then drafted the design on a 4" grid. As we looked at the sharp points of the leaves and carrots, it became apparent that paper-piecing was the best method of construction. Some of the blocks are very intricate, such as where the flower leaves pass behind the carrot and radish leaves. However, by paper-piecing you are able to keep the points accurate and sharp.

INSTRUCTIONS
❀ McGREGOR'S GARDEN

❀ MATERIALS

Refer to the photograph for color placement. Yardage amounts allow for the trimming necessary in paper-piecing construction.

Background
- 5 yards total of a variety of muslin tones
- 1 yard total of a variety of pink tones
- 5/8 yard total of a variety of lavender tones
- 5/8 yard total of a variety of very pale yellow tones

- Carrot: 1/3 yard for body, 2/3 yard each of two colors for leaves
- Radish: 1/3 yard for body, 2/3 yard each of two colors for leaves
- Tulip: 1/4 yard for center, 1/4 yard for top, 1/2 yard for sides, 1/2 yard for stem, 1 yard for leaves
- Allium: 1/3 yard for center, 1/4 yard for outside, 1/3 yard for stem, 1/2 yard for leaves
- Backing: 5 2/3 yards
- Batting: 84" x 100"
- Binding: 1/2 yard

❀ CUTTING

Cut 4 1/2" squares from the following color groups: 132 muslin, 24 yellow, 20 pink, and 28 lavender. Use the leftover fabric in the background of the paper-piecing blocks.

Strips and small cuts of yardage are more workable when paper-piecing. Cut 40" strips on the crosswise grain to use in the paper-piecing for the flowers, leaves, and vegetables.

Tulips
sides: five 1 3/4" wide
center: four 1 3/4" wide
top: two 2 1/2" wide
stem: five 1" wide
leaves: thirteen 2" wide

Allium
center: two 1 1/2" wide
outside: three 1 1/2" wide
stem: three 1" wide
leaves: three 2 1/2" wide

Carrot
body: four 2 1/2" wide
dark leaves: fourteen 1 3/4" wide
bright leaves: eleven 1 3/4" wide

Radish
body: two 5" wide
dark leaves: fourteen 1 3/4" wide
bright leaves: eleven 1 3/4" wide

❀ BASIC GUIDELINES FOR PAPER-PIECING

The finished block will mirror the traced pattern, which was allowed for in producing the patterns.

As you work, stitch on the lined side of the paper. Before trimming the blocks, add 1/4" seam allowance beyond the edge of the paper.

Do not be concerned with the grain of the fabric. You are stitching on paper, which stabilizes the block. The paper will not be torn off until after the blocks are stitched together.

Set the stitch length on your machine to 18 to 20 stitches to the inch. Follow the number sequence when piecing. Some of the patterns are pieced in sections, then the sections joined together (illustrations are included for these blocks). After piecing the block, trim the raw edges to 1/4" beyond the edge of the paper.

✿ DIRECTIONS

Photocopy the patterns (pages 132-138) on a good copy machine to minimize distortion. You will need fourteen each of carrots and radishes, six each of the right and left sides of the allium, and ten each of the right and left side of the tulips. I always make one extra copy of everything. It may be helpful to photocopy the quilt illustration and prepare a mock-up of your fabric choices to use as a guide.

1. Start by cutting a piece of fabric 1/2" larger than the finished section. (Count the number of blocks you will be making, then cut the total you will need.)

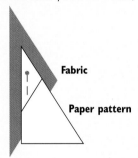

Fabric

Paper pattern

2. Lay the fabric piece, right side down, on the table. Place the foundation paper on top of the fabric with 1/2" fabric around the paper. Pin in place. To double check, turn the paper over and you should see the right side of the fabric.

3. Before adding the second fabric, fold the paper foundation on the stitching line. Place the second fabric on the first with right sides together and matching raw edges.

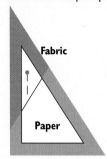

Fabric

Paper

Fold

Unfold the paper and check to see if the second fabric extends beyond the seam allowances. Keep the 1/2" extra fabric around the edges so you have plenty to work with. Pin in place. In some instances strips of fabric have been cut to go with the odd-shaped pieces.

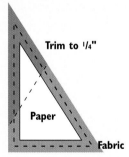

Fabric

Paper

4. Stitch through the paper and the two fabrics using the line on the paper as a guide. Fold back the paper and trim the seam allowances to 1/4". Unfold the paper, open the fabrics flat, and trim the outside seam allowances to 1/4" beyond the edge of the paper.

Trim to 1/4"

Paper

Fabric

5. This process will seem tedious at times but the results are accurate and dramatic. The process will go faster if you complete each section at once: all of the tulips, then all of the leaves, etc.

6. Note that on the radish and carrot leaves in the corners of the quilt have background areas treated as a single piece of fabric. Make four each. Subtract this from the total amount listed.

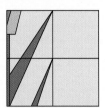

Make 4 Left Tulips

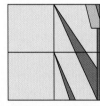

Make 4 Right Tulips

Make 4 Carrots each

Make 4 Radishes each

7. Arrange four rows of eight 4" squares each for the center of the quilt. Stitch squares together in rows, and then join the rows. Arrange lavender squares around the center. Stitch two sets of four squares together and add a set to each short end of the center. Stitch two sets of ten squares together and add a set to the long sides of the center section.

8. Tear off the paper foundation when you are ready to add a section to the quilt. Because the quilt is planned on a 4" grid, you have seams that match up every four inches and this stabilizes the quilt. Use the illustration as a guide for the assembly of the rest of the quilt. This method is similar to adding a series of pieced borders to construct a quilt.

✿ FINISHING

Refer to the Batting and Layering instructions on page 13. The simple gridded quilting pattern enhances the open spaces in the quilt and makes the design livelier. The pieced vegetables and flowers are outlined. Refer to the Binding instructions on page 13.

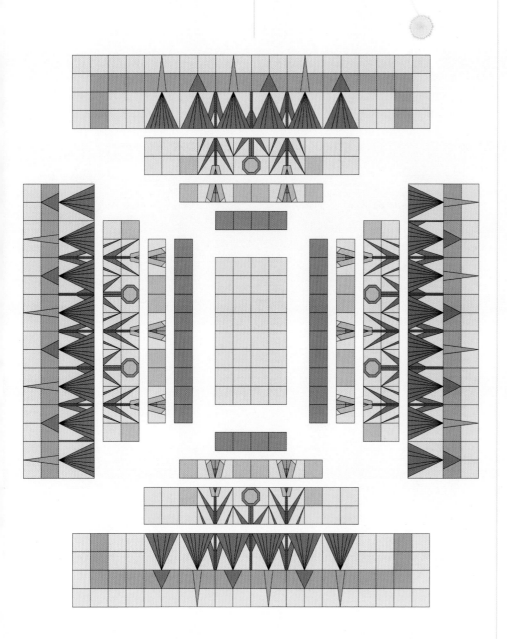

CAROL FARNES:

Carrol Clark ~ Garden Helper

Preserving an Open Space

in the City for All to Share

Gardening nourishes the soul. "It is easy to lose track of time and the demands of the outside world when I am working in the garden. The garden is my little piece of heaven right here on earth." With these words, Carol Farnes captures the sentiment of all of the gardeners featured in *Through the Garden Gate*.

Carol and her husband purchased a full city lot which meets the street next door to her home. They began the task of transforming the hillside property into a city garden to be shared by all. Huge rocks were brought in and the structure began. The garden "guest book" holds signatures from Poland, France, and Singapore as well as states as far away as New York, Tennessee, and Texas.

"Welcome to the Garden" signs greet the visitors with gravel pathways directing traffic through the garden "rooms." Her latest room incorporates a tropical look with huge leaves and tall plants like hibiscus, cannas, castor beans, and Joe Pye weed, to name just a few. Other rooms feature perennials found in English cottage gardens; a rock garden with sedums; tall sunflowers; and an archway covered in hops. The garden is full of unique, hard-to-find plants like the blue poppy.

Gathering plants is a favorite pastime for Carol, as is knowing the name of every single plant in the garden. After reading about a special plant in one of the many gardening publications she subscribes, her quest might lead her to an interesting nursery, or she may receive "starts" or seeds from friends. Thank-you notes from visitors sometimes contain tiny packets of hand-collected and carefully labeled seeds from their gardens. Years ago, the early springtime would find Carol starting seeds in her living and dining room window sills, but now she has a greenhouse for these tasks.

Nature spontaneously creates some wonderful combinations. Seeds blow to another area, sprout, and find new neighbors that lead to new combinations in the garden. Maybe it is a squash vine with its enormous leaves which appeared in a bed of flowers or a sunflower that grew much too close to the path, causing visitors to duck as they went by. This touch of whimsy adds to the charm of the garden. Copying these effects in quilting leads to spontaneity in the use of color.

Creativity and patience are necessary for both quilters and gardeners. It often takes years for an area to develop, just as it does for quilting ideas. Color and surprises make the spontaneous part of gardening that inspires Carol in her quilting.

In summer, Carol hosts garden tours to raise money for her favorite charities. The tea party table pictured was inspired by an article in the June 1997 *Sunset* magazine. With the help of her gardening friend, Carrol Clark, she placed sod on a plastic-covered table with ivy tacked around the edge. (These two recommend rolling out the grass a week ahead and watering it.) Mow if necessary before placing on the table. Pansy dishes and accessories complete the table arrangement.

In the garden the eye is led from one area to another by the use of texture as well as color. Gravel pathways wind past boulders draped in flowers with a hop-covered archway in the distance. Silvery greens are reflected next to deep dark greens as flower colors abound. There are areas to sit on a bench and reflect upon what you are seeing and sensing and to marvel at the effort and creativity that has gone into this city garden setting.

Repeating what has been done before is not a goal of this gardener. A saying from her mother "If at first you don't succeed, try and try again" serves her well. Consequently she is never afraid to try something new if it's creating something exciting.

Quilting and cultivating the garden are only two of her interests. Together, the two gardeners harvest and dry almost everything from the garden. The garage is brimming with pods, flowers, and foliage that will find their way into wreaths or bouquets.

Garage sales and estate sales provide interesting containers and backdrops, such as old windows, which lend themselves to interesting arrangements.

Enchanted Morning

Butterflies, birds, spiders, dragonflies, and bumblebees enhance this *Enchanted Morning* quilt. A 3" grid forms the backdrop of the quilt with 1 1/2" Four-Patches replacing the 3" squares at random to create an interesting background. Notice how Carrol uses the softer lights in a variety of tones toward the top of the quilt. The colors gradually get darker as they reach the ground yet still stay light to medium-light in comparison to the rest of the composition.

By piecing the lighter background in subtle value changes creates more interest without overwhelming the appliqué images. The fabric choices for the appliqués are medium and medium dark values with a few brights. This contrast shows up well.

Gardens seem to draw unexpected visitors from time to time, like the rabbit and the frog. Butterflies and an occasional dragonfly appear in the early-morning scene. Adding cosmos and fox-glove vines creates a mystical early morning scene. All are part of Mother Nature's plan.

The appliqué shapes are fused in place with paper-backed adhesive, and then the vines, stems, and leaves are topstitched with the sewing machine. The shapes were then hand button-hole stitched to complete the design.

CARROL CLARK

Quilted by Katrina Beverage

50 1/4" x 50 1/4"

INSTRUCTIONS

ENCHANTED MORNING

❀ MATERIALS

- 1 3/4 yards total of assorted lights and medium lights for pieced background
- 1/2 yard each of two different greens for vines, stems, and leaves
- 6" x 12" scrap for birds
- 7" x 9" scrap for rabbit
- 5" x 6" scrap for frog
- 1/8 yard of two fabrics for daisies
- 5" x 8" scrap for cosmos buds
- 1/8 yard for cosmos
- 5" x 9" scrap for cosmos and daisy centers
- 1/4 yard for foxgloves
- Scraps of fabrics for butterflies and other bugs
- 1/4 yard for first border
- 1/2 yard for second border
- 3 1/2 yards for third border, binding, and backing
- 54" x 54" batting

- 4 yards paper-backed adhesive
- one each of black and gold six-strand embroidery floss or #8 pearle cotton thread
- one each of silver, gold, and black embroidery thread
- five $1/8$" buttons for eyes on appliqués
- two $1/2$" googly eyes for frog
- optional lady-bug button

✿ CUTTING

QUILT

Cut a few extra squares for the background so you will have a choice when determining placement of the squares: One hundred thirteen 3 $1/2$" squares for the companion patches.
One hundred forty 2" squares for the thirty-five Four-Patches.
Cut two 3 $1/2$" squares for the corner triangles, then cut diagonally.
Cut eight 5 $1/2$" squares for setting triangles, then cut diagonally in both directions for a total of twenty-nine needed.

For first border: cut two 1 $1/4$" x 38 $3/4$" strips for the sides. Cut two 1 $1/4$" x 40 $1/4$" strips for the top and bottom.
For second border: cut two 2 $1/2$" x 40 $1/4$" strips for the sides. Cut three 2 $1/2$" x 40" strips, then stitch together lengthwise. Cut two 42 $1/4$" long for the top and bottom.
For third border: cut four 3 $1/2$" x 42 $1/4$" strips (if your fabric isn't 43" wide you will need to piece the strips). Cut four 3 $1/2$" squares from the second border fabric for corners.

APPLIQUÉ SHAPES

Note that the appliqué shapes will reverse themselves once they are fused in place. Appliqué patterns are found on pages 138-143. Trace the following on the paper side of the paper-backed adhesive:

Dragonfly A (1), Dragonfly B (1), Bumblebee (5), Grass (3), Worm (1), Cosmos (5), Cosmo buds (8), Foxglove (10 mixing the three sizes to create flowers), Foxglove buds (7 mixing the three sizes), Butterfly A (1), Butterfly B (1), Frog (1), Birds (1 of each), Daisy (9), Leaves (11 small and 20 medium), Large leaves (2 each of a, b, c, d), Cosmo and foxglove vines (3 each of a, b, c, d, e, f), Daisy stems (two $1/2$" x 40" strips, refer to the photograph for trimming), Rabbit (1)

✿ DIRECTIONS

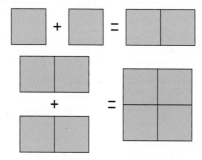

Four-Patch, 3" Finished block

QUILT

1. Arrange background squares, setting triangles, and corner triangles on a design wall, starting with the lighter colors at the top and graduating to the medium lights at the bottom. Insert the Four-Patch blocks at random to create an interesting background. Some of the Four-Patch blocks and companion patches will become bottom setting triangles and will need to be trimmed off. When you are satisfied with the design, sew together the Four-Patch blocks. Press.

2. Stitch the blocks in each row together in a diagonal set, and press. Join row 1 to 2, etc, and press.

3. Add the side strips of the first border, then the top and bottom. Press. Repeat for second border.

4. Add the side strips of the third border. Stitch the corner blocks to each end of the top and bottom strips, then add to the quilt. Press.

APPLIQUÉ SHAPES

1. Select fabrics for all of the appliqués. Following the manufacturer's instructions, fuse the paper-backed adhesive to the wrong side of the fabric, then cut the shapes.

2. Add vines, stems, leaves, and rabbit to the quilt top first, referring to the photograph for placement. Fuse the shapes following the manufacturer's instructions. Machine straight stitch $1/16$" from the edge of the vines, stems, and leaves only.

3. Place the remaining appliqués on the quilt, remembering that you are designing a garden and can move things around if you wish. You may add or subtract the appliqués.

4. Buttonhole stitch the other shapes in place. (You may use a machine blanket stitch, but these appliqués were hand stitched.)

To buttonhole stitch, use two strands of floss or one of pearle cotton. Knot the end of the thread. Working from the fabric back, pull the needle up at the edge of the appliqué. Insert the needle through the appliqué about $1/8$" from the edge.

(This distance will vary with the size of the appliqué.) Emerge parallel to the appliqué edge, bringing the needle tip over the working thread. Pull the stitch into place until the thread along the edge is secure and slightly taut.

Hold the working thread with your left thumb and take another stitch. Repeat the process to continue stitching. Keep the stitches proportional to the motif. The width of the stitch can vary as well as the length.

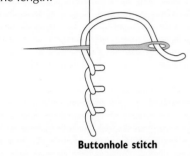

Buttonhole stitch

As you approach a narrow point, emerge with the needle tip at the top edge of the point, then insert the needle back into the fabric, as if you are ending the stitch. This tacks the stitch in place. Bring the needle up again a couple of fabric threads over (shown with the dot in the illustration) and start stitching again.

EMBELLISHMENT

1. Attach the 1/8" buttons for the eyes on the birds and rabbit, and the 1/2" googly eyes for the frog.

2. To create the spider web, thread two strands of silver thread and one of black in a large needle. Place the structure lines first, radiating from the center, similar to spokes on a wheel. Connect to the flower stems just as a real spider web would look.

Join the spokes by bringing the needle up beside a spoke, tacking over the spoke, and then stitching to the next spoke.

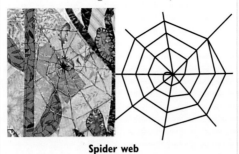

Spider web

3. For the spider body, stitch three large French knots close together, using black embroidery floss or pearle cotton thread. Add one French knot for the head, then stitch eight straight stitches out from the body for the legs.

To make a French knot, knot the end of the thread. Working from the fabric back, pull the needle up to the fabric top. Wrap the needle twice with the working thread, then insert the needle back into the fabric, as close to the first stitch as possible. Pull the stitch into place until the thread is secure and slightly taut.

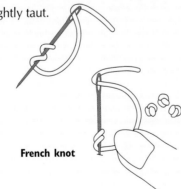

French knot

4. For the stripes of the bee's body, thread six strands of gold floss, stitching over the body and head with a straight stitch. Add French knots for eyes, using black embroidery floss or pearle cotton thread.

5. On the butterfly and worm, thread two strands of black floss and stem stitch the antennae. Straight stitch the legs.

To stem stitch, knot the end of the thread. Working from the fabric back, pull the needle up to the fabric top. Working from left to right, insert the needle into the fabric parallel to the first stitch and emerging midway between the stitch points. Pull the stitch into place, keeping the needle over the working thread.

Stem stitch

6. Sew a lady-bug button on the flower of your choice.

✿ FINISHING

Refer to the Batting and Layering instructions on page 13. For the quilting, lines resembling vines were stitched vertically to mimic the foliage. Each appliqué shape was outline stitched since it is too difficult to stitch through bonded fabric. Refer to the Binding instructions on page 13.

Summer Garden

Sawtooth Star blocks placed on point create a floral mood in *Summer Garden*. Dominant in this quilt are blocks made to resemble the red hibiscus flowers grown from a friend's seeds, which came into their own this year. Sunflowers are always a focal point in any garden, and they also appear in Carol's quilt. She chose the Sawtooth Star block and set it on point to create a grid in which to work her colors.

Carol uses a method she calls "create and place as you go" to form the blocks. Each unit in the block is treated as a separate piece on the design wall. A neutral backdrop for the vibrant reds and yellows is formed by a variety of greens, from deep dark to lighter sage and cream. The reverse sides of fabric were used to "blur" the transition from cream to deeper green. This is a watercolor-quilt trick which works well in other floral quilts.

Blending colors through gradual changes of different fabrics is similar to painting with fabric. Carol discovered new quilting talents in herself as she machine quilted *Summer Garden*. To give the quilt a feeling of the garden, she sketched simple foliage shapes and then free-motion quilted them at the bottom of the quilt.

CAROL FARNES
82 1/2" x 88 3/8"

❀ SUMMER GARDEN

❀ MATERIALS

A variety of different fabrics are used in each unit of the star blocks. Total yardage amounts are given within color ranges, but the number of different fabrics you choose in each color is up to you.

- 3 3/8 yards total for cream background
- 3 yards total of greens
- 1 yard total of reds
- 3/4 yard total of yellows
- 3/8 yard for the first border
- 1 1/3 yards for the second border and binding
- 6 yards for backing
- 86" x 92" batting

❀ CUTTING

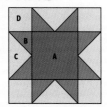

Sawtooth Star, 8" Finished

Carol cut fabric as she composed the star blocks. You may also choose to cut as you go.

A: One hundred five centers are needed for the blocks. The squares should be cut 4 1/2". If you want to split some of the squares to create more interest, cut a square of fabric 4 7/8" then cut it diagonally.

B and C: Together, these pieces make a unit for the star points. Notice that a variety of fabrics are used.

Cut three hundred sixty-four 2 1/2" x 4 1/2" rectangles for **C**. Cut seven hundred twenty-eight 2 1/2" squares for **B**.

D: Cut three hundred ninety-one 2 1/2" squares.

For the first border, cut eight 1 1/2" strips, then stitch the strips together lengthwise. Cut sides 80 3/8", and the top and bottom 76 1/2".
For the second border, cut eight 3 1/2" strips, then stitch the strips together lengthwise. Cut sides 82 3/8", and the top and bottom 82 1/2".

❀ DIRECTIONS

1. The **B** and **C** unit consists of double half-square triangles. Fold **B** in half diagonally then lightly press the fold. You will need two of **B** for each unit. Place the right side of **B** onto a short end of **C** and stitch along the fold line, diagonally across the **B** square. Trim away excess, as shown, leaving a 1/4" seam allowance. Open the triangle and press. Repeat for the other side of **C**.

Fold in half diagonally, press

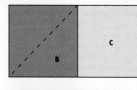
Trim

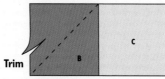

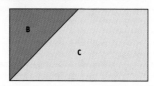

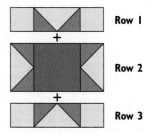
Trim

2. Once four **B** and **C** units are complete, stitch the block together as shown. Complete 105 blocks for the quilt. Press.

Row 1
+
Row 2
+
Row 3

3. Stitch the blocks together in rows in a diagonal set, joining row 1 to row 2, etc. Press.

4. Trim the quilt edges straight. Because the blocks are set on point, some of the blocks will be cut in half along the edges.

5. Run a line of stay-stitching a scant 1/4" away from the raw edges on all four sides of the quilt to stabilize the edges.

6. Add the first border, stitching the sides first, then the top and bottom. Repeat for the second border. Press.

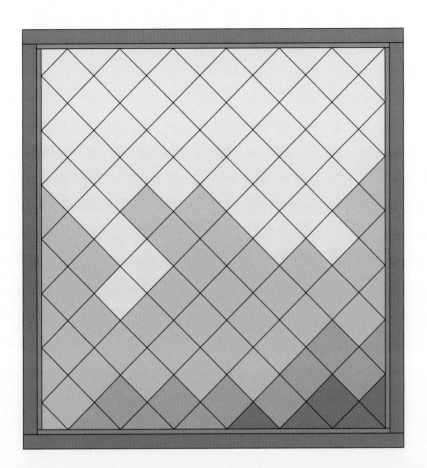

✿ FINISHING

Refer to the Batting and Layering instructions on page 13. Carol used a combination of stippling and plant shapes in quilting the quilt. Sketches of the plants are given on page 123 if you choose to enlarge them 200% on a copy machine and use them for your quilting design. Refer to the Binding instructions on page 13.

Although I have been surrounded by gardening and quilting my entire life, I still consider myself an amateur. Working on this book has inspired and encouraged me to find my own path in both. It has been an extraordinary experience photographing and interviewing the wonderful quilters and gardeners within this book. I have been led down the personal and spiritual paths that lie with this experience. They opened their gates and hearts to me. I feel very lucky to have been a part of this book and to have glimpsed into such creative expression.

Valori Wells

ABOUT THE AUTHORS

Jean and Valori Wells have teamed up again to write and photograph *Through the Garden Gate*. Working together seems to bring out the best in both of these talented women.

Gardening is a second love for Jean. In the past eighteen years she has transformed a sandy slope with pine and juniper trees into a garden paradise with a variety of plants, trees, and shrubs. Valori grew up observing and participating in the design and planting of this special environment, which made creating *Through the Garden Gate* a labor of love and sharing for this talented mother/daughter team.

Jean Wells is the owner of The Stitchin' Post and The Wild Hare in the small mountain community of Sisters, Oregon. For the past twenty-four years she has not only run a successful quilt shop but has also written over eighteen how-to quilting books, and has contributed numerous

articles for magazines, designed two fabric lines for P&B Textiles, appeared on several televised quilting programs, and taught business and quilting workshops throughout the U.S. and Europe. In 1998 she was one of the first "Independent Retailers" to be inducted into the Primedia Hall of Fame. At the 1998 Houston Quilt Show, Jean Wells received the Michael Kile Award for Lifetime Achievement in the industry.

Valori Wells is a recent graduate of the Pacific Northwest College of Art and received the "Outstanding Photographer for 1997" award. Free-lancing as a nature and portrait photographer gives Valori a variety of photography experiences. Quilting has been added to her list of creative endeavors along with printmaking and papermaking. Valori has been exploring quilt design, combining photo transfer and piecing techniques.

SOURCES

Calico Hills Farm Patterns
8292 Redstone Ave. SE
Salem, OR 97306
503-581-6272

Dennis McGregor Design
PO Box 736
Sisters, OR 97759
541-549-1128

Gwen Marston (books)
PO Box 155
Beaver Island, MI 49782
616-448-2565

The Stitchin' Post
Jean Wells (owner)
PO Box 280
Sisters, OR 97759
541-549-6061

For quilting supplies:
Cotton Patch Mail Order
3405 Hall Lane, Dept. CTB,
Lafayette, CA 94549
e-mail: cottonpa@aol.com
(800) 835-4418
(925) 283-7883

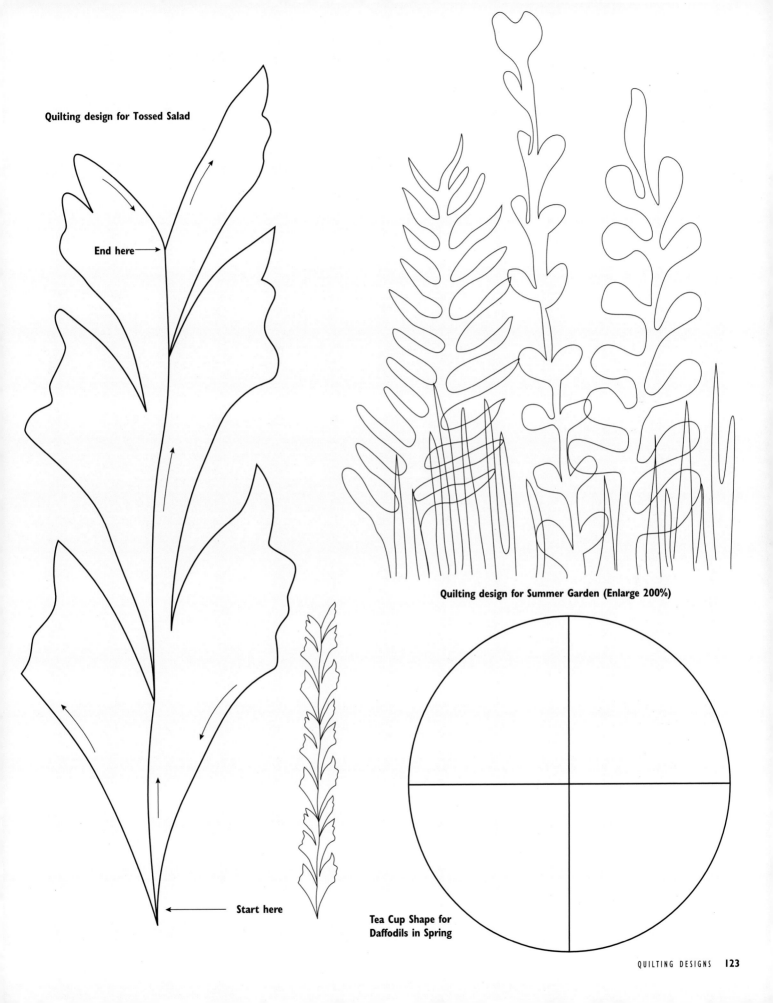

Quilting design for Tossed Salad

End here →

Start here

Quilting design for Summer Garden (Enlarge 200%)

Tea Cup Shape for
Daffodils in Spring

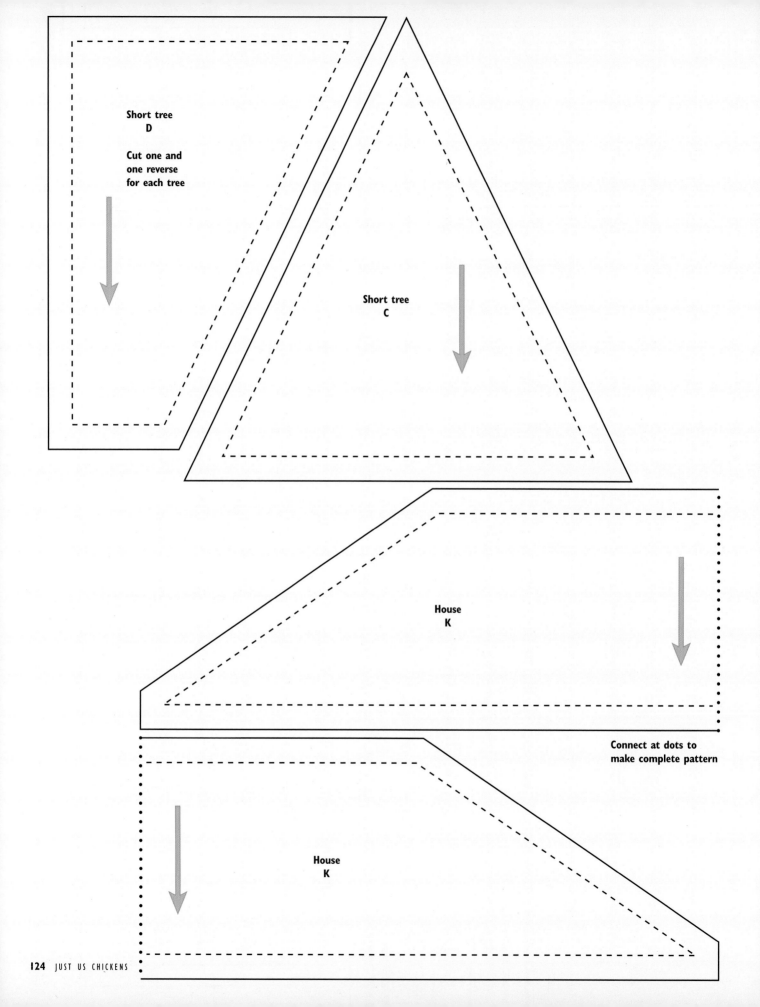

Short tree
D

Cut one and
one reverse
for each tree

Short tree
C

House
K

House
K

Connect at dots to
make complete pattern

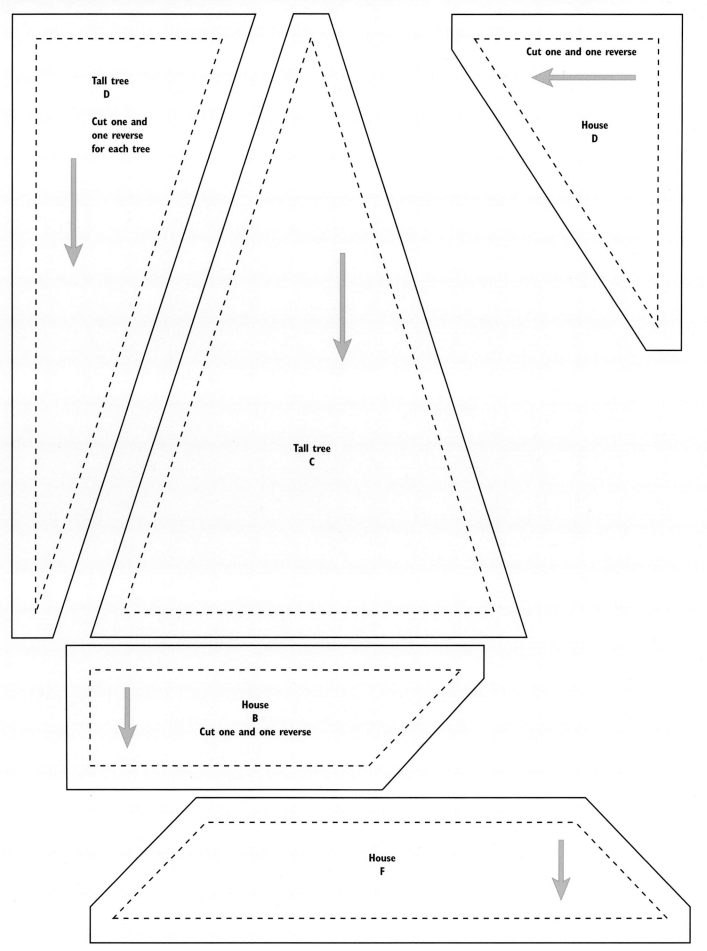

Tall tree
D

Cut one and
one reverse
for each tree

Cut one and one reverse

House
D

Tall tree
C

House
B
Cut one and one reverse

House
F

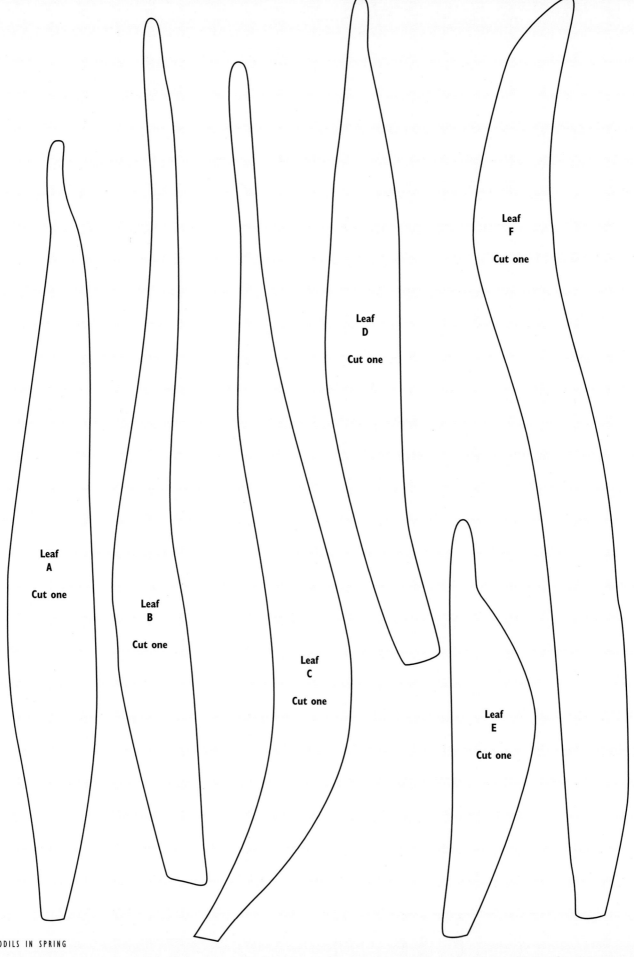

Leaf
A

Cut one

Leaf
B

Cut one

Leaf
C

Cut one

Leaf
D

Cut one

Leaf
E

Cut one

Leaf
F

Cut one

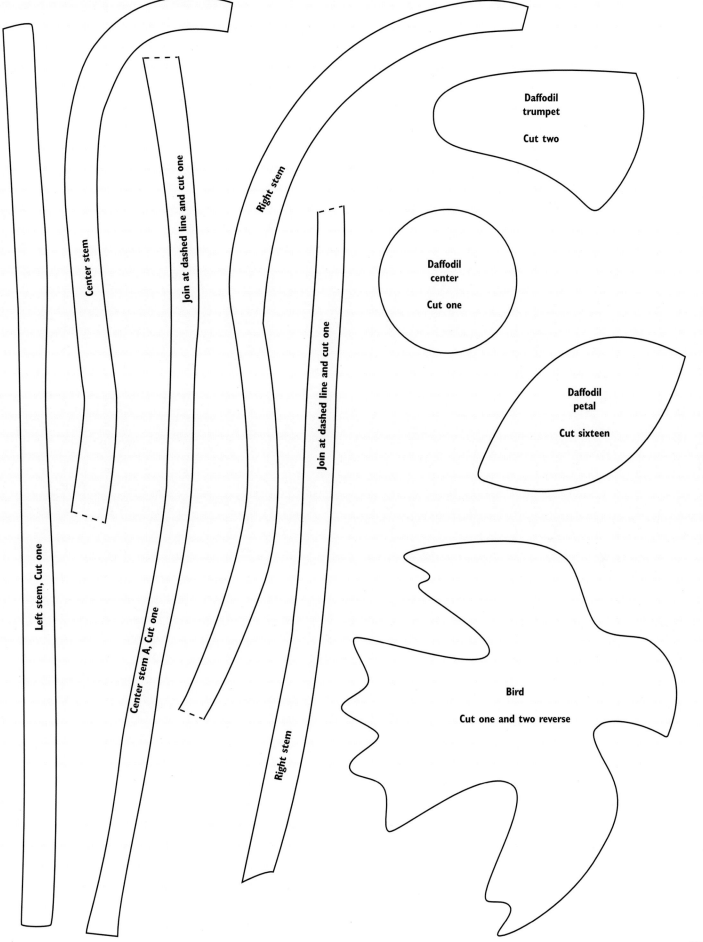

Center stem

Join at dashed line and cut one

Right stem

Left stem, Cut one

Center stem A, Cut one

Join at dashed line and cut one

Right stem

Daffodil trumpet

Cut two

Daffodil center

Cut one

Daffodil petal

Cut sixteen

Bird

Cut one and two reverse

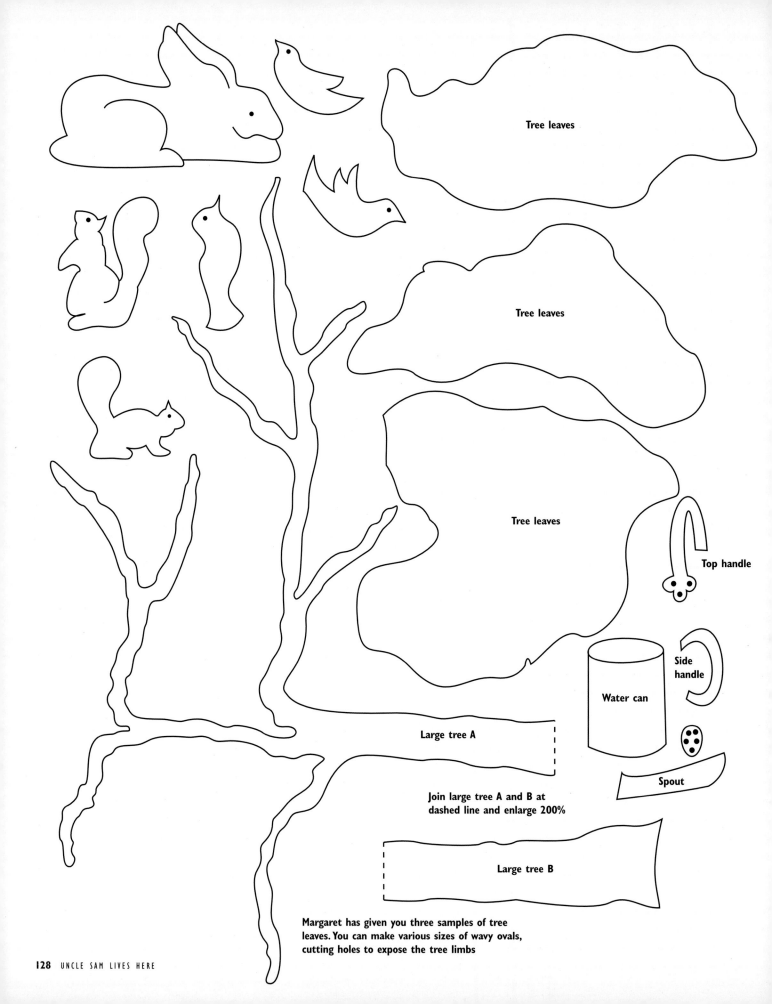

Tree leaves

Tree leaves

Tree leaves

Top handle

Side handle

Water can

Spout

Large tree A

Join large tree A and B at
dashed line and enlarge 200%

Large tree B

Margaret has given you three samples of tree
leaves. You can make various sizes of wavy ovals,
cutting holes to expose the tree limbs

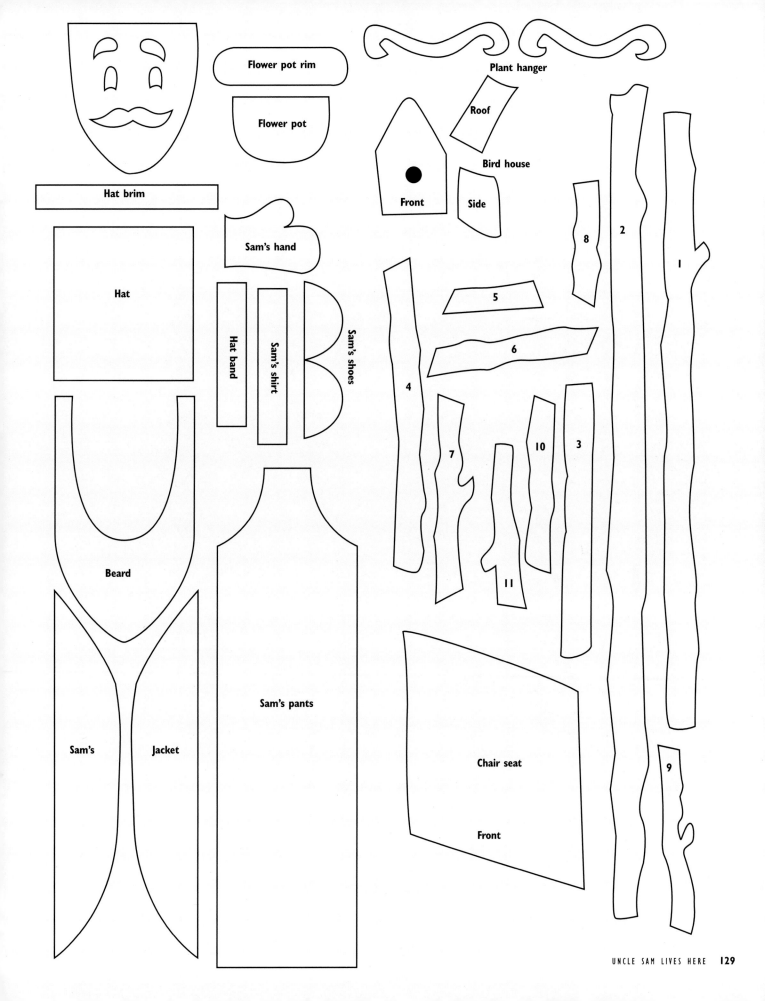

Flower pot rim

Flower pot

Plant hanger

Roof

Bird house

Front

Side

Hat brim

Hat

Sam's hand

Hat band

Sam's shirt

Sam's shoes

Beard

Sam's

Jacket

Sam's pants

4

8

2

1

5

6

7

10

3

11

9

Chair seat

Front

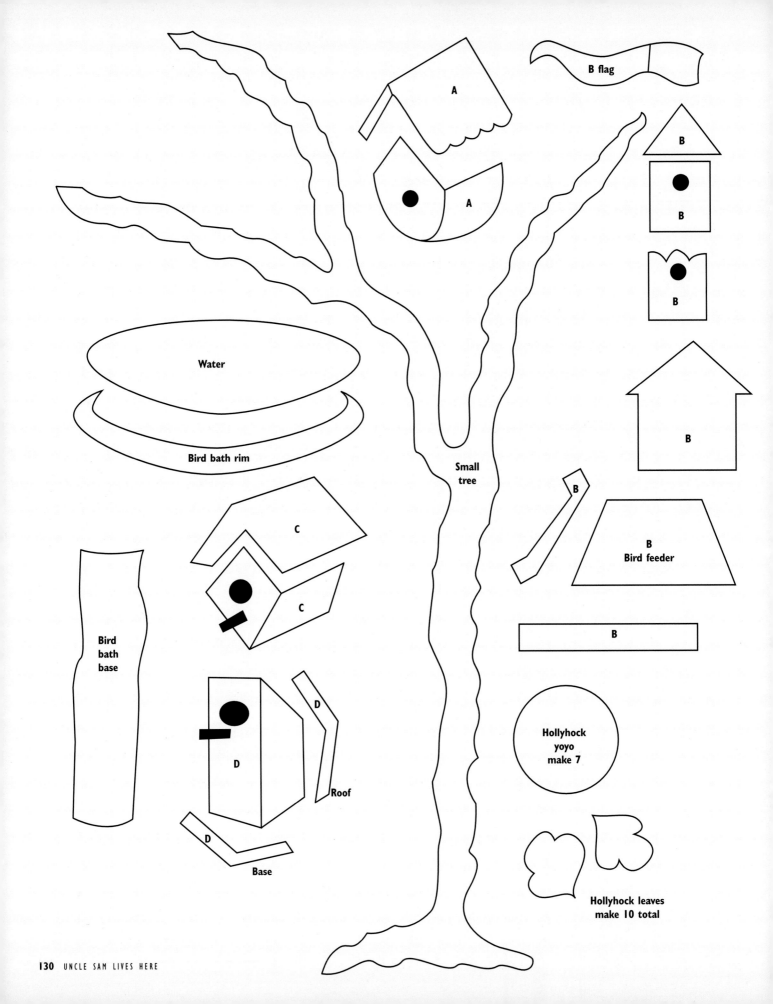

A

B flag

B

B

B

B

Water

Bird bath rim

Small tree

B

B
Bird feeder

B

C

C

Bird bath base

Hollyhock yoyo make 7

D

D

Roof

D

Base

Hollyhock leaves make 10 total

Enlarge block quilting designs 200%

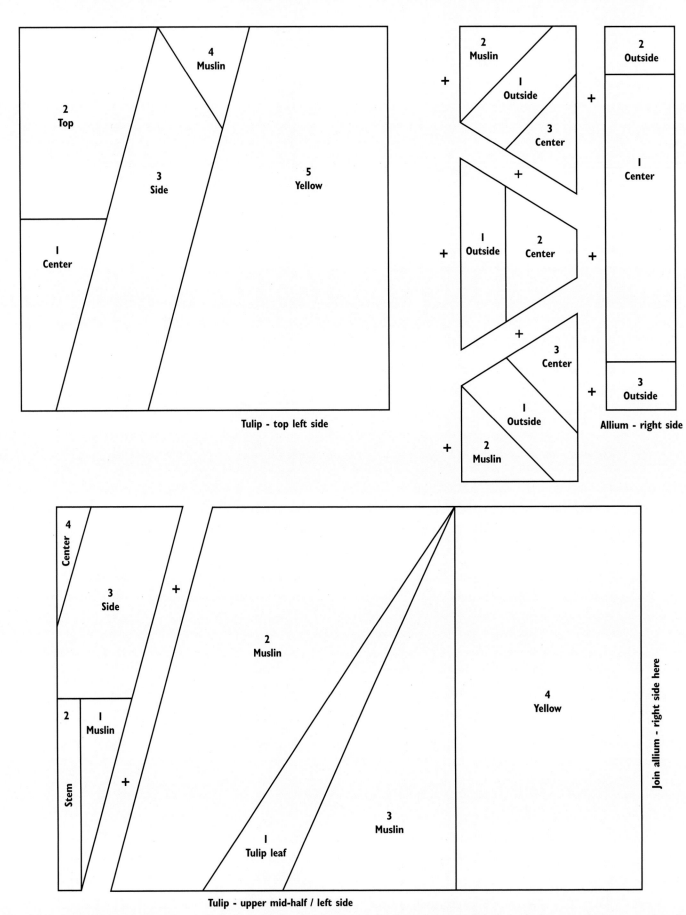

2
Top

4
Muslin

3
Side

5
Yellow

I
Center

Tulip - top left side

+

2
Muslin

I
Outside

3
Center

+

2
Outside

I
Center

3
Outside

+

+

I
Outside

2
Center

+

+

3
Center

I
Outside

+

2
Muslin

+

Allium - right side

4
Center

3
Side

+

2
Muslin

2

I
Muslin

Stem

+

I
Tulip leaf

3
Muslin

4
Yellow

Join allium - right side here

Tulip - upper mid-half / left side

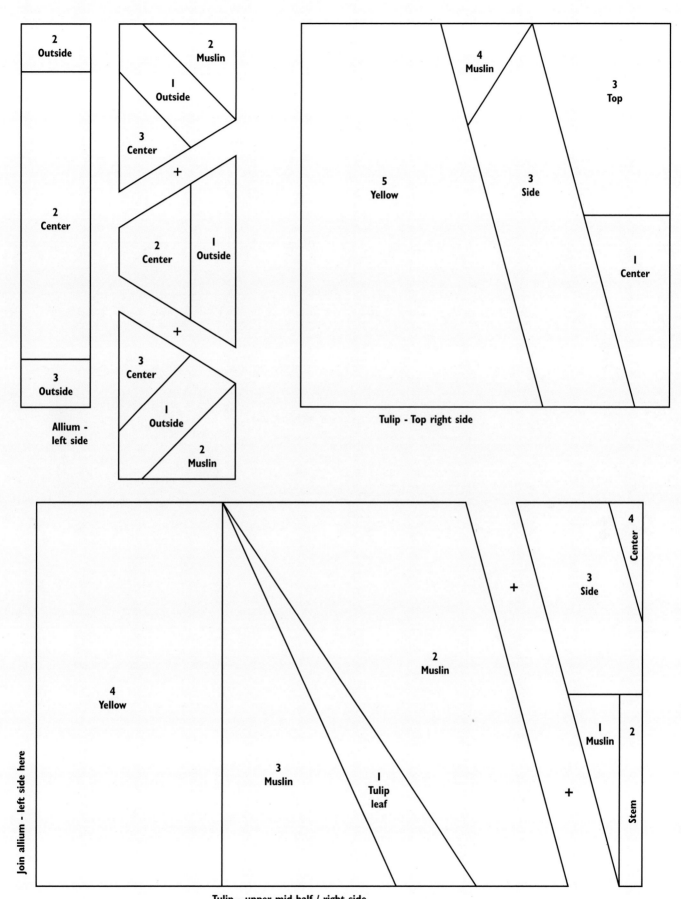

2
Outside

2
Center

3
Outside

Allium -
left side

2
Muslin

1
Outside

3
Center

+

2
Center

1
Outside

+

3
Center

1
Outside

2
Muslin

4
Muslin

3
Top

5
Yellow

3
Side

1
Center

Tulip - Top right side

Join allium - left side here

4
Yellow

3
Muslin

1
Tulip
leaf

2
Muslin

+

3
Side

4
Center

1
Muslin

2

Stem

+

Tulip - upper mid-half / right side

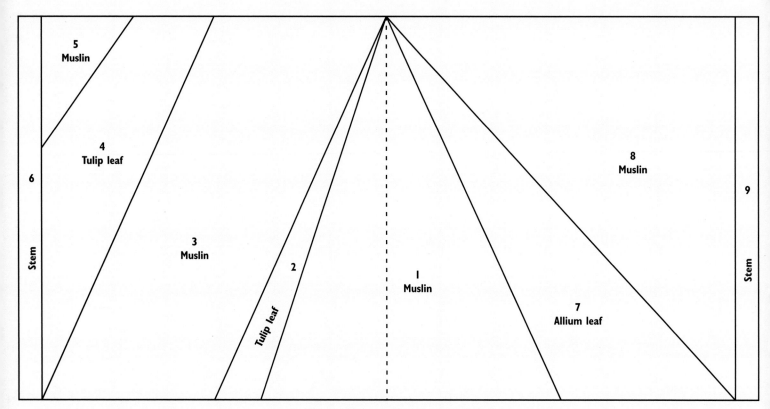

Tulip / Allium - lower mid-half / left side

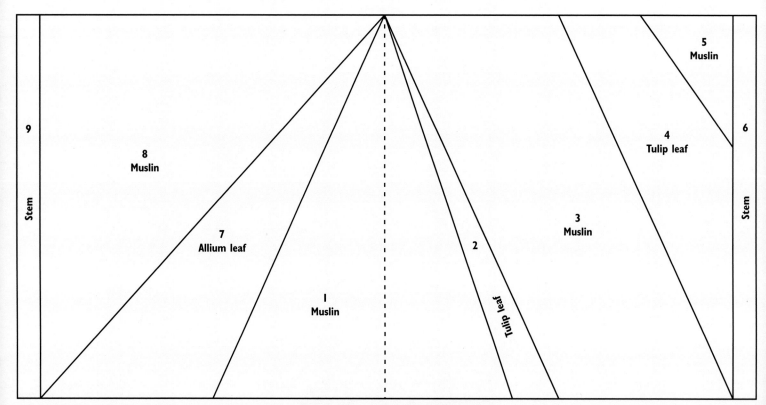

Allium / Tulip - lower mid-half / right side

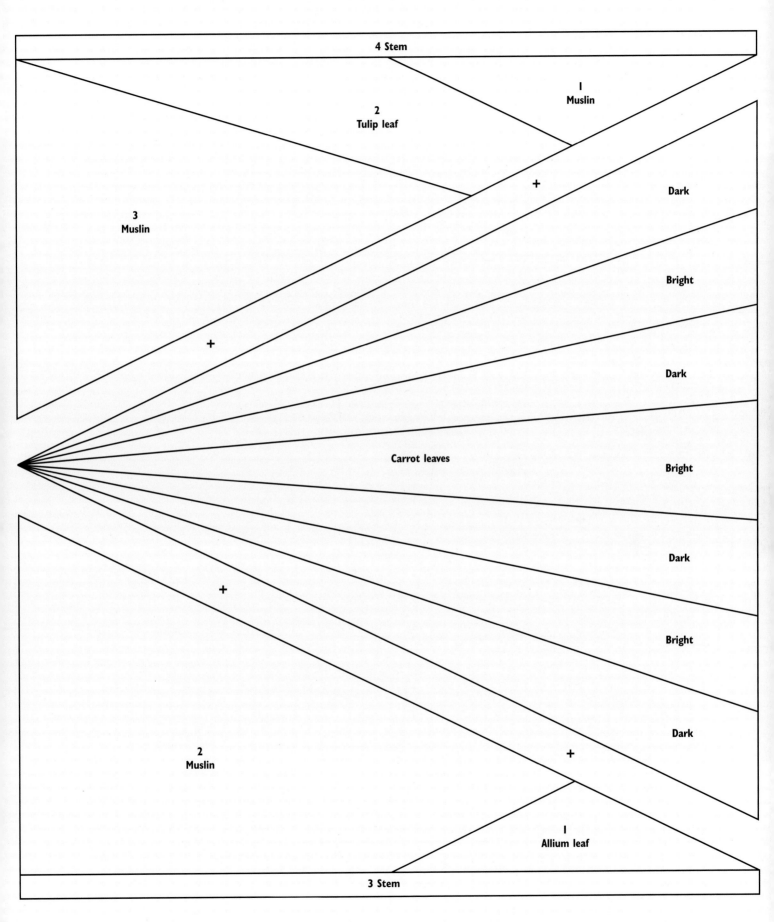

4 Stem

1
Muslin

2
Tulip leaf

3
Muslin

+

Dark

Bright

+

Dark

Carrot leaves

Bright

Dark

+

Bright

Dark

+

2
Muslin

1
Allium leaf

3 Stem

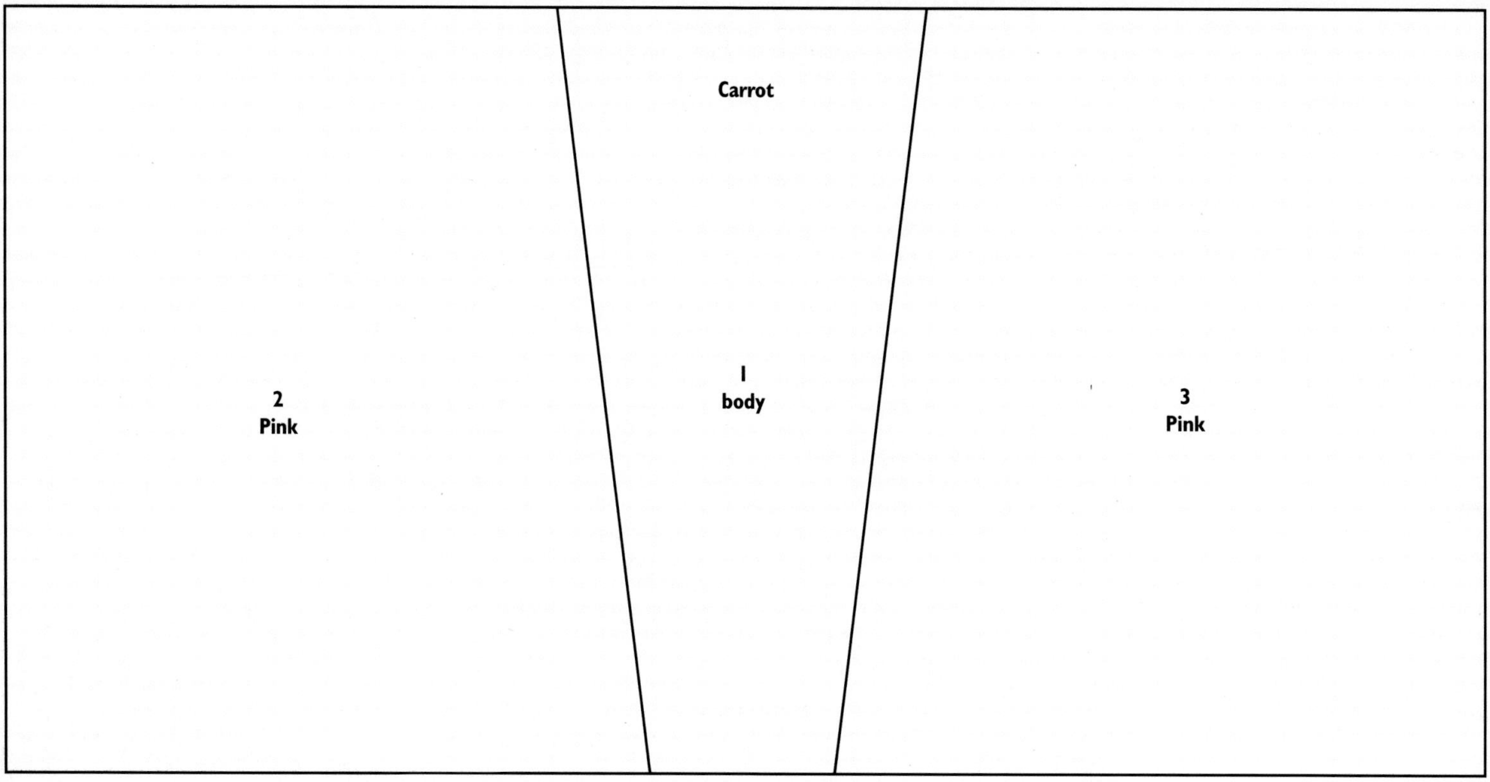

Carrot

2
Pink

1
body

3
Pink

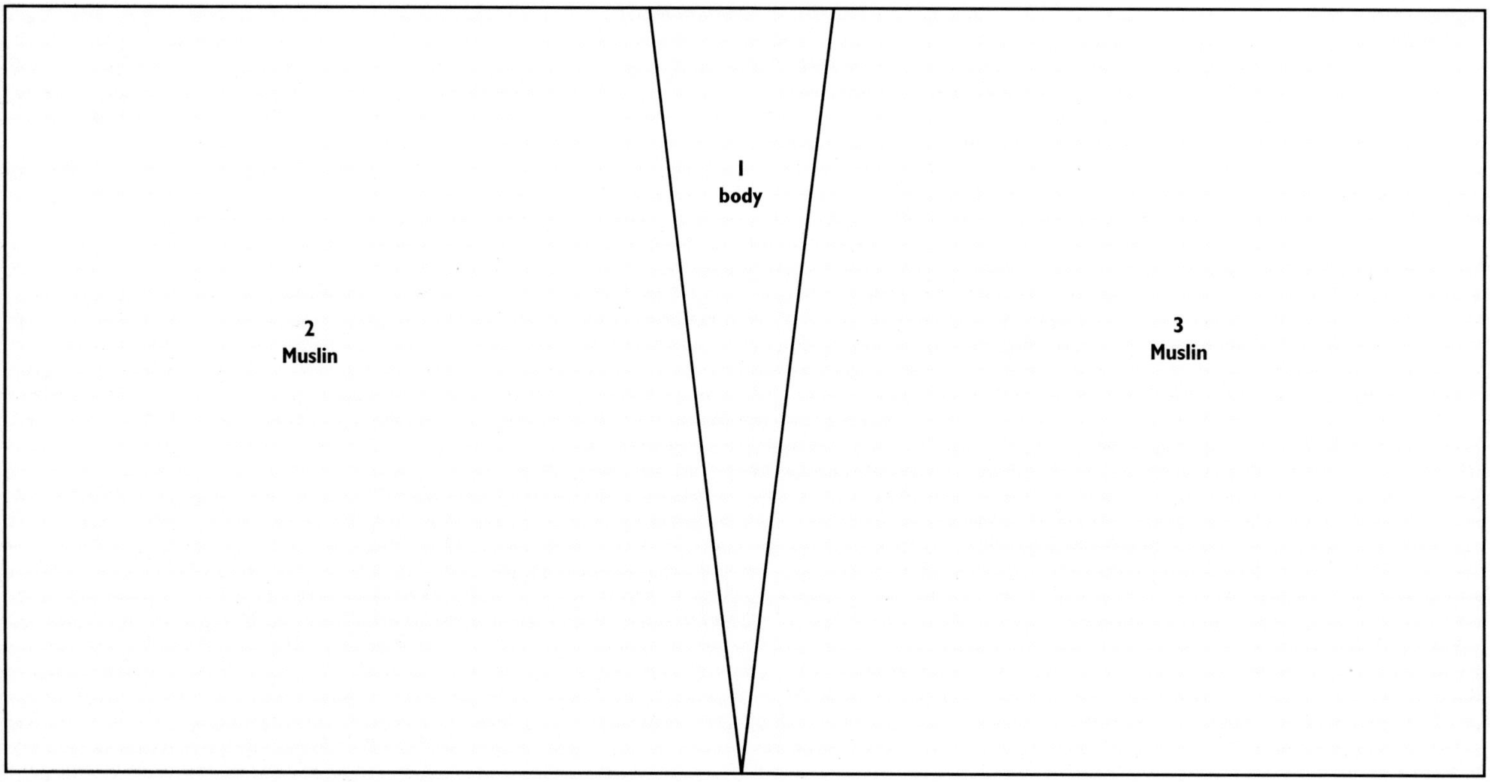

1
body

2
Muslin

3
Muslin

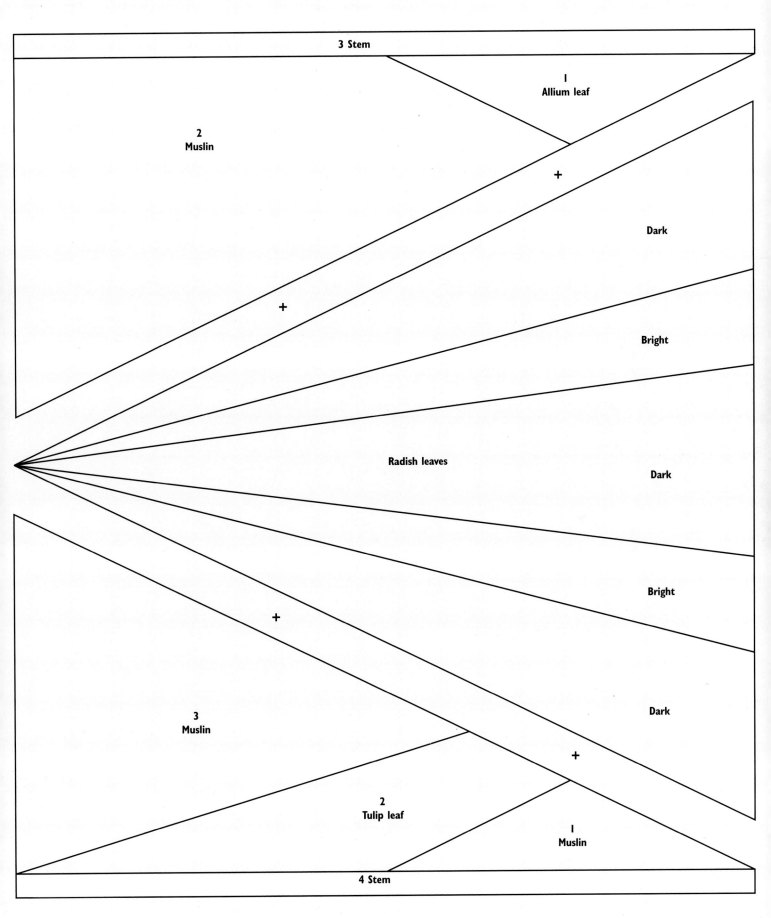

3 Stem

I
Allium leaf

2
Muslin

+

Dark

+

+

Bright

Radish leaves

Dark

Bright

+

3
Muslin

Dark

+

2
Tulip leaf

I
Muslin

4 Stem

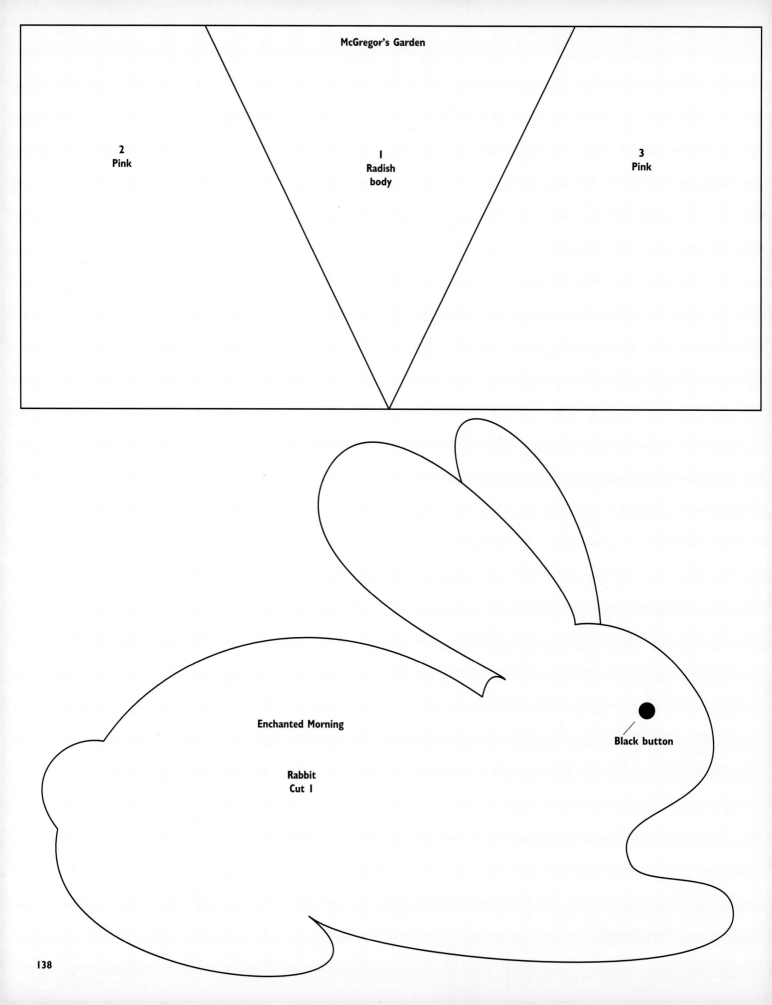

McGregor's Garden

2
Pink

I
Radish
body

3
Pink

Enchanted Morning

Black button

Rabbit
Cut I

138

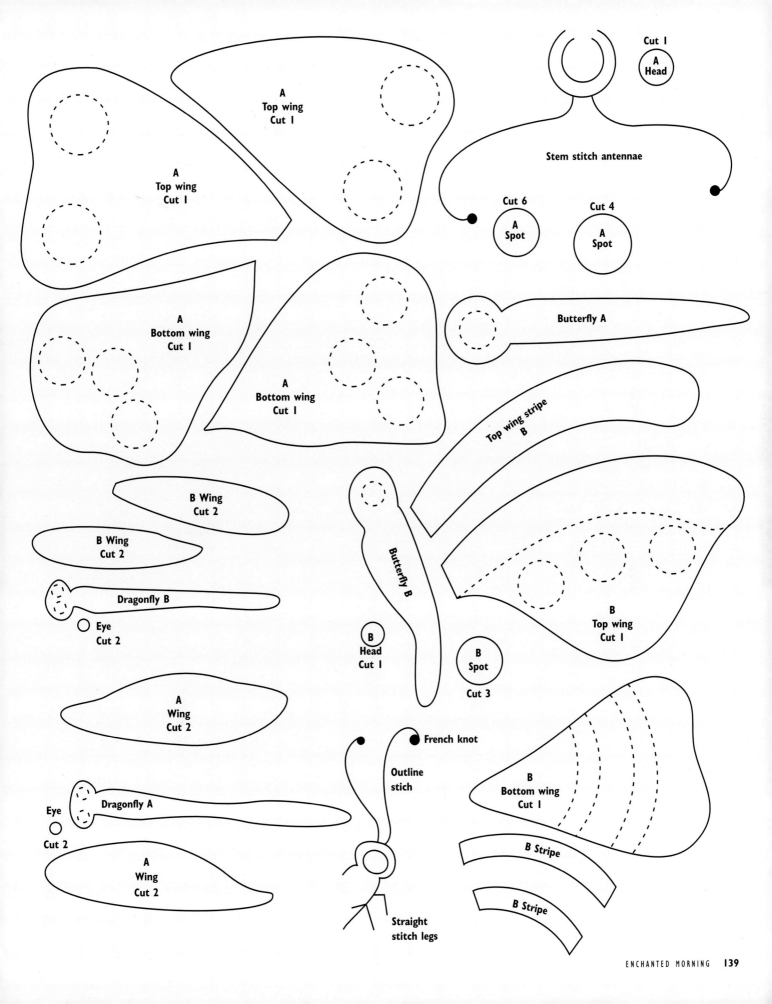

A
Top wing
Cut 1

A
Top wing
Cut 1

Cut 1
A
Head

Stem stitch antennae

Cut 6
A
Spot

Cut 4
A
Spot

A
Bottom wing
Cut 1

A
Bottom wing
Cut 1

Butterfly A

Top wing stripe
B

B Wing
Cut 2

B Wing
Cut 2

Butterfly B

B
Top wing
Cut 1

Dragonfly B

Eye
Cut 2

B
Head
Cut 1

B
Spot
Cut 3

A
Wing
Cut 2

French knot

Outline
stich

Eye

Dragonfly A

B
Bottom wing
Cut 1

Cut 2

A
Wing
Cut 2

Straight
stitch legs

B Stripe

B Stripe

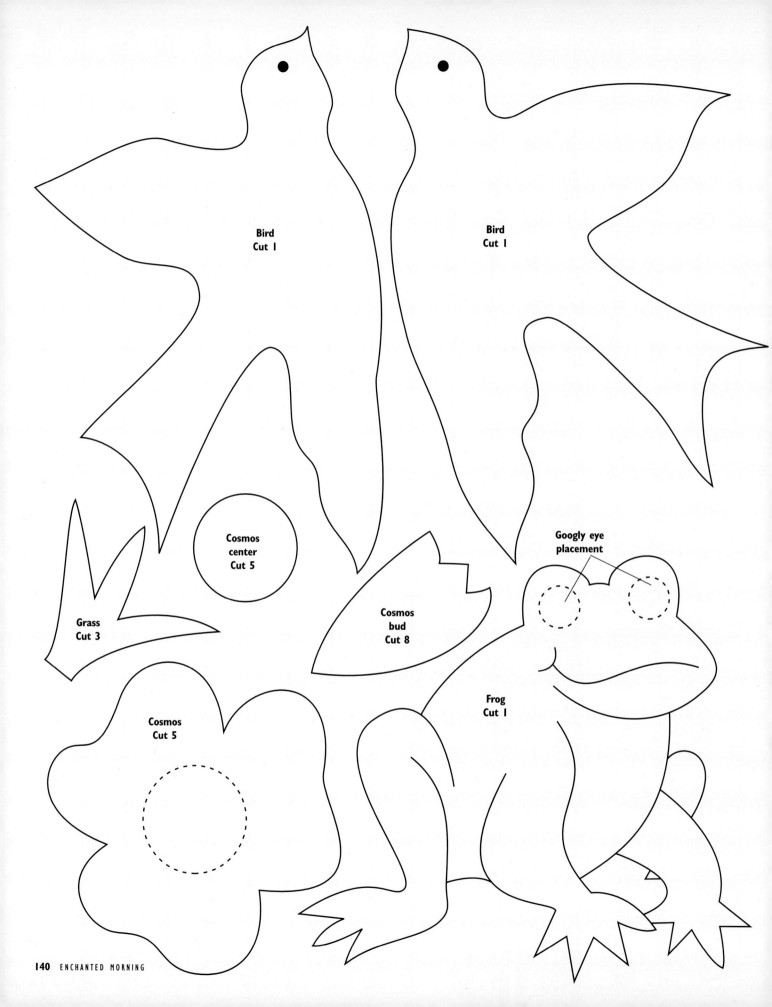

Bird
Cut 1

Bird
Cut 1

Cosmos
center
Cut 5

Grass
Cut 3

Cosmos
bud
Cut 8

Googly eye
placement

Cosmos
Cut 5

Frog
Cut 1

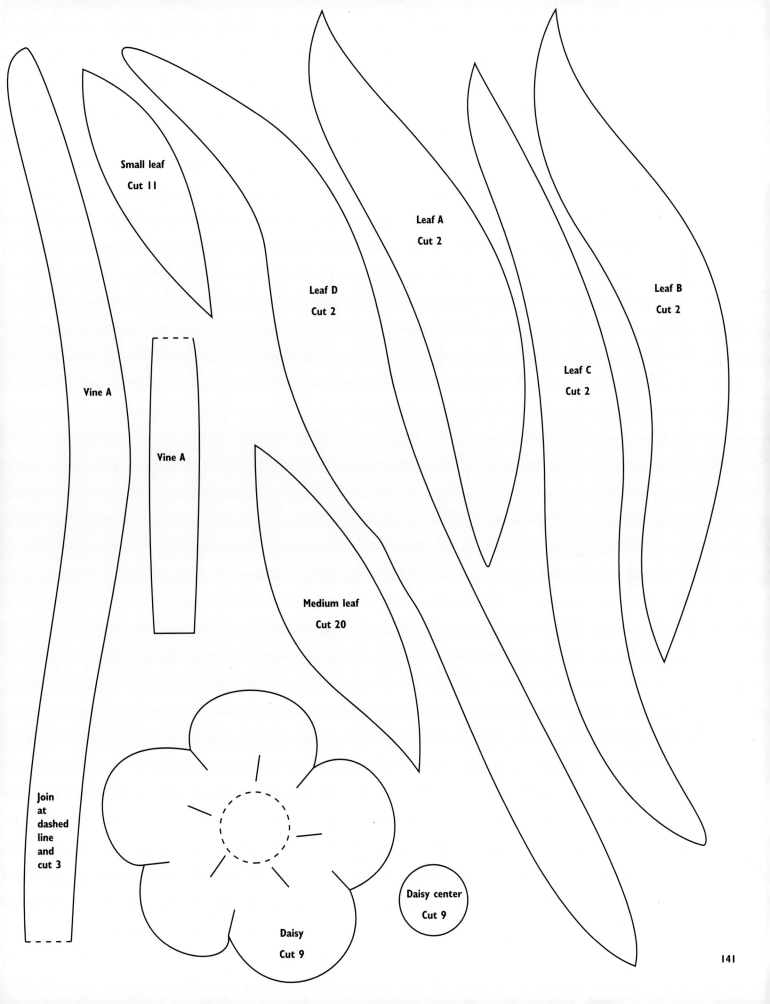

Small leaf
Cut 11

Leaf A
Cut 2

Leaf D
Cut 2

Leaf B
Cut 2

Leaf C
Cut 2

Vine A

Vine A

Medium leaf
Cut 20

Join
at
dashed
line
and
cut 3

Daisy
Cut 9

Daisy center
Cut 9

141

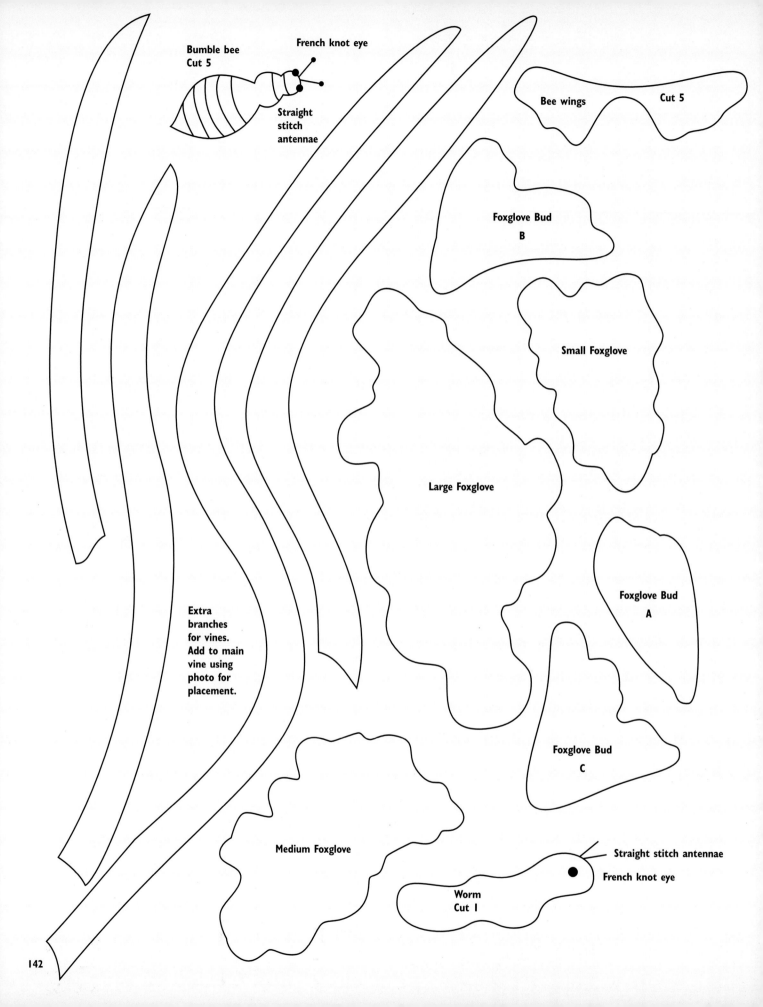

Bumble bee
Cut 5

French knot eye

Straight
stitch
antennae

Bee wings   Cut 5

Foxglove Bud
B

Small Foxglove

Large Foxglove

Foxglove Bud
A

Extra
branches
for vines.
Add to main
vine using
photo for
placement.

Foxglove Bud
C

Medium Foxglove

Straight stitch antennae

French knot eye

Worm
Cut 1

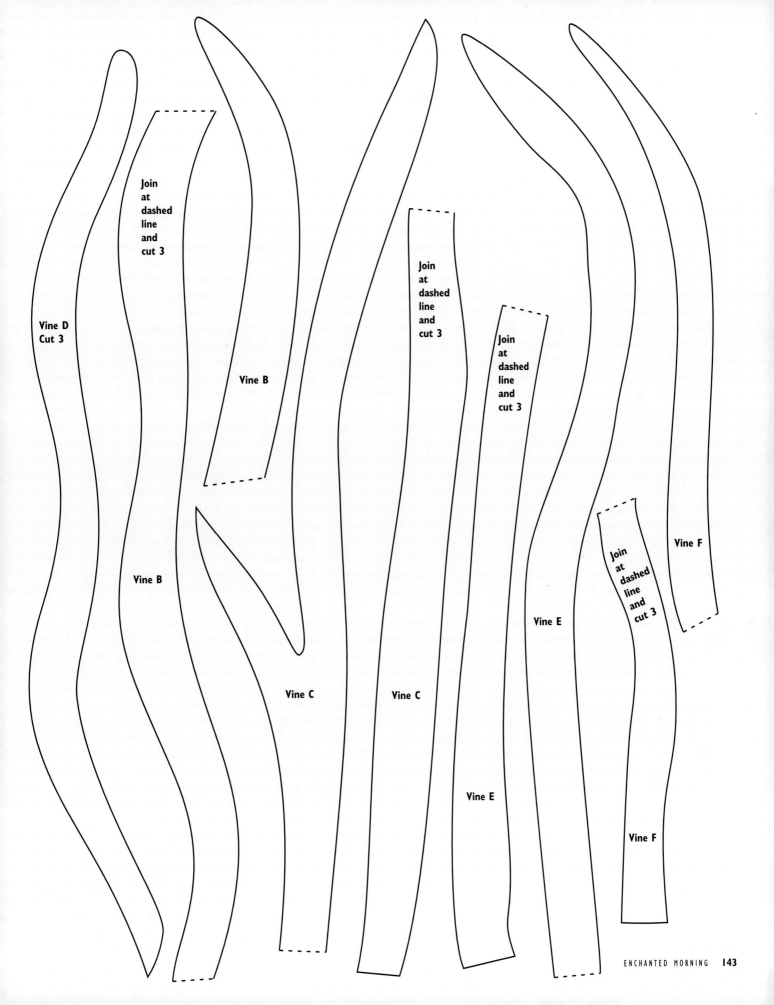

Vine D
Cut 3

Join
at
dashed
line
and
cut 3

Vine B

Vine B

Vine C

Join
at
dashed
line
and
cut 3

Join
at
dashed
line
and
cut 3

Vine C

Vine E

Join
at
dashed
line
and
cut 3

Vine F

Vine E

Vine F

 # INDEX

Other favorites by Jean and Valori Wells from C&T Publishing, Inc.: